HAVE FUN OUT THERE

OR NOT

THE SEMI-RAD RUNNING ESSAYS

AND RACE REPORTS, AND SOME FUNNY
LISTS, AND SOME DRAWINGS

BY BRENDAN LEONARD

Copyright © 2022
Brendan Leonard/Semi-Rad Media
All rights reserved.
ISBN: 978-0-578-37671-4

For Jayson Sime, who is really to blame for all of this

CONTENTS

	Introduction	1
1	Surviving a 4K (4,000-Calorie) Run	5
2	The Suffer Vest	11
3	The Ice Age Trail 50	21
4	Happiness Is Your Backyard Trail	27
5	The Run Rabbit Run 100	31
6	The Rim-to-Rim-to-Rim: A Trail Diary	41
7	A New York Pizza Marathon	51
8	Why Finish Lines Will Get You Every Time	57
9	Fear And Groaning At The Hellbender 100	63
10	A Case For The Apple Fritter As Endurance Fuel	79
11	The Hill That You Love To Hate	85
12	The Bighorn 100: A Race Report	89

13	We Are Running Nowhere	105
14	Marathon Tips From My Friend Syd	109
15	How To Go For A Run In 22 Simple Steps	113
16	52 Marathons In A Year	117
17	Winter Running Tips For Masochists	129
18	The Year Of Making Your Own Fun Run	135
19	Solitaire	151
20	Post-Workout Recovery Methods That Haven't Been Proven To Work …Yet	173
21	26 Useful Facts About Running	179
22	Going Fast, Going Far	185
23	"Parking Lot Laps": A Rationale	191
24	Race Report: The Rut 50K	209
25	My Friend Says It's The Greatest Race In The World	223

INTRODUCTION

I would like to get one thing out of the way before you start reading the stories in this book: I am not a lifelong runner. I did not run cross-country in high school (although I did run short-distance events on the track team). I didn't run in college, and when I say I didn't run, I don't mean "I did not run on a college track or cross country team." I mean I worked as a janitor and then a bartender, and picked up a pack-a-day smoking habit that lasted six years. I eventually quit smoking and got in good enough shape to run a marathon in 2006, and I did not think it was fun, so I took nine and a half years off running.

Then I got really into it when I was in my 30s, sucked in by the mystique of ultramarathon running. The things I experienced and learned are in the pages of this book. Several hundred jokes are also in this book, because no matter how many miles I run, I have not lost sight of the fact that it's a bit of a ridiculous hobby.

When I started putting my writing and drawings online at Semi-Rad.com in 2011, I thought of myself primarily as a climber—rock climbing, mountaineering, usually most excited when I was carrying a rope and wearing a helmet. Several years into an ultramarathon phase of life, I realized I had done a lot of writing about running—enough to fill a book. So I took what I thought were the best 25 pieces and made this book out of them.

I don't really stretch, or do track workouts, or keep a training diary, or have a coach—although I have friends who do those things and they're great people, and usually faster than me (which makes me think those things might be good ideas—especially stretching). I just like going out there and wandering around, at a pace faster than walking. I run by myself most of the time and spend a lot of time in my own head, and when I do run with friends, we run slowly enough that we can talk the whole time.

I'm not trying to pretend I'm cool because I don't take running seriously—I take it seriously, just in other ways. I have, to this date, finished every ultramarathon and marathon I've entered, knock on wood, and that requires a substantial amount of giving a shit. But I also spend a lot of that solitary ultramarathon time thinking up funny things to say to the next person I see, who is usually someone working at an aid station. A few examples:

- "How far am I behind the leaders?" (late in a race, when the leaders have quite obviously finished hours before me)
- "Do you work here? I would like to speak to a manager." (everyone here is volunteering, there is no manager, this is a race, not an Applebee's)
- "Hey, I am pretty sure I signed up for the 10K race. Did I miss a turn?" (more ridiculous the further into a race you are; i.e. Mile 50 or later)

I would like to think there are things we all have in common as runners, no matter what speed we run, or how long it takes us to finish a race. I hope I captured some of that in these pages.

With that said, the first essay is about a few guys each eating about 4,000 calories' worth of bagels, pizza, cheesecake, donuts, and other foods, while (slowly) running about 21 miles across New York from Harlem to Coney Island in the July heat, which I feel is kind of appropriate.

Thanks for reading.

1

SURVIVING A 4K (4,000-CALORIE) RUN

In 2013, I pitched Outside Magazine *a story about running a sort of "food marathon" in New York City—running 20-plus miles, eating iconic New York foods all along the way . They said yes, assigned me a 1,000-word story, and I wrote it. After a lot of back and forth, the story was cut to basically a map that appeared in an issue of the magazine and then online. So, a few years later, I decided to edit the original draft a little bit and publish it on my website.*

--

When Forest and I had discussed the rules at a coffee shop in Brooklyn three days earlier, I had said, "I think vomiting is allowed."

"I think vomiting is advised," he said.

I wonder how many bad ideas start with two grown men asking each other "What if we ..." This one ended with "ran around New York eating all the most awesome food in one day?"

The idea had come up at the apartment of my friend Syd, a lifelong New Yorker. Sitting at his kitchen table with a copy of *Zagat's New York City Food Lover's Guide 2012-2013* and a smartphone between us, we compiled a list of classic New York foods, and the best place to get each of them. Our list had to be defensible: each restaurant had to have a legitimate claim to being the best in the city. Some were easy; picking the best pizza was not. We broke a five-way tie by picking Totonno's because it was the furthest away from the others, thus requiring the most running, upping the suffer factor by nine additional miles.

The final list:

- Best Bagel: Absolute Bagels, Upper West Side
- Best Egg Cream: Eisenberg's Sandwich Shop, Flatiron District
- Best Knish: Yonah Schimmel Knish Bakery, Lower East Side
- Best Hot dog: Katz's Delicatessen, Lower East Side*
- Best Street Pretzel: Sigmund's Pretzels, East Village
- Best Donut: Doughnut Plant, Lower East Side
- Best Cheesecake: Junior's, Brooklyn
- Best Pizza: Totonno's Pizzeria Napolitano, Coney Island

Then Syd got injured, aggravating a tear in his calf muscle. I worried if he'd heal in time to train for the New York Marathon in 16 weeks. He was heartbroken he wouldn't be able to run around with Forest and me, Harlem to Coney Island, bagel to pizza. He chose to run the middle eight miles or so and subway the rest, enabling him to eat everything but the bagel.

I'd heard stories about the cashier at Absolute Bagels at Broadway and 108th, 500 feet from Harlem. One Yelp reviewer called her a "dragon." People said words like drill sergeant, rude, Soup Nazi. She is the boss, and has no time for your dawdling. Know what you want, tell the guys behind the counter your order, then tell her your order again, pay, and get out of the way. The line of hungry customers winds out the door here for most of the morning every day of the year. At 8:05 a.m., we began. I ordered two of the best bagels I've ever had. Forest asked, "Two?" and I thought, Indeed, Forest, why am I eating two bagels at the beginning of a day of nonstop eating. Then I ate both of them anyway.

I figure 10-minute miles, I told Forest as we jogged down 108th into Central Park, turning right onto West Drive, joining the hundreds of joggers and walkers getting in their Sunday morning workout. The first of the more than 3,000 New York City Triathlon participants passed us going the other way, grinding through the race's 10K running leg after their 1500-meter swim in the Hudson River and a 40K bike ride on the Henry Hudson Parkway. It was 90 degrees.

We poured sweat immediately, stopping to fill up water bottles at a fountain on the south side of the park, and left the green of Central Park behind to jump onto the wide sidewalks of the just-waking-up Sixth Avenue, trying to stay on the shady side of the street. We passed Radio City Music Hall, bumped over to Fifth Avenue under the Empire State Building, then ducked into Eisenberg's Sandwich Shop across the street from the Flatiron Building, to leave sweat marks on the counter seats and knock out an icy egg cream apiece.

Out of curiosity, I asked a friend of a friend about running nutrition: Craig Strong, USA Triathlon Level II coach and founder of Chicago-based Precision Multisport, said when it comes to long-distance running, a guy my size (5'11", 180 pounds) should eat before running, then shoot for 100 to 125 calories per hour of running. Twenty-one miles at 10 minutes per mile is roughly 3½ hours of running, so four GUs could pretty much cover our run from Harlem to Coney Island.

"You could do 21 miles on a sports drink," Strong says. "You're not going to run out of protein, and you're not going to run out of fat." A knish, a street pretzel, and a doughnut totals about 1,300 calories, in about 12 blocks of running. We estimated our total intake at about 4,000 calories for the day, and Forest jokingly called our run "a 4K."

At the water fountain at Katz's, Josh Hirsch, owner of a tour company called Sidewalks of New York, asked me, "Are you guys running from restaurant to restaurant?" They had seen us running out the door of Yonah Schimmel, and now at Katz's. I said yes, we were, and he explained that he was leading a group on a walking food tour of the Lower East Side.

"That sounds a lot smarter," I said. At every food stop, Forest hashtagged his photos #eat #run #vom.

Syd religiously runs the NYC Marathon every year, and last year, he told me he spent 13 minutes of his total race time stopping to talk to people. "I think if you're going to run a marathon, you should try to high-five as many people as possible," he said. This is why Syd and I are friends. If you can either try to run with the most speed possible, or the most fun possible, I choose fun. And donuts and cheesecake.

Which is way more fun on paper, and an entirely new sports challenge when you've just eaten a knish, hot dog, and a street pretzel in about an hour and are running through Chinatown in the July heat. People run laps around Central Park, not through Chinatown, because: smells of fish, garbage, exhaust, street vendors cooking; dodging pedestrians and food carts and the occasional delivery truck.

We weaved through bicycles and walkers up and over the Brooklyn Bridge, then ran up Flatbush Avenue to duck into Junior's for the air conditioning and a slice of the best cheesecake in the city, 550 calories. Nine miles to go. Eating I had trained for; running, I had not.

Through Prospect Park, then down 4 ½ miles of Ocean Parkway toward Coney Island. We walked into Totonno's Pizza, a pizzeria aware of its reputation as one of the best in New York: It's no-frills, with paper plates, open only until the dough runs out. Three of us easily dispatched two large, immaculately sauced, coal-fired cheese pizzas, easily pushing us over 4,000 calories for the day. Afterward, no one suggested we jog over to Nathan's Famous for one of the most legendary hot dogs in New York, only four blocks away. But we did ride the Cyclone at Coney Island, impressively with no #vom.

2

THE SUFFER VEST

This piece came into existence because of an email from Jen Altschul, a longtime producer and writer for the podcast The Dirtbag Diaries, *asking "Want to write something for us?" I had done a few stories over the years, and loved the storytelling format. I had just run my first ultramarathon, the Bear Chase Trail Race 50K in Lakewood, Colorado, and thought it might make for a fun story. When I was writing it, the biggest question I had for Jen, Fitz, and Becca at* The Dirtbag Diaries *was: Can you get the rights to play a few seconds of the Beastie Boys' "Rhymin and Stealin"?*

--

I have band-aids covering my nipples, two water bottles with bright red bite valves strapped to my chest, short shorts on, and lubricant on the insides of my thighs and small of my back. As I clip the front buckles on the vest and grab both water bottles like a pair of boobs, I think to myself, Wearing this vest is the second dumbest thing I'll do today.

Twenty-four days earlier, I sat across the table from my friend Jayson in a Denver pizza restaurant and listened to him tell me about how he epiced on a 27-mile run in the heat that morning, having to stop and beg hikers for water after he ran out near the tail end of his training run. Jayson was training for his first ultramarathon, the Bear Chase Trail Race. He was limping a little. It sounded horrible. I started to get a small headache just from listening to him describe it.

The next morning, I got out of bed and ran 10 miles. I don't know why. Just to see if I could. That afternoon, I signed up for my first ultramarathon, the same one Jayson was doing. It was a 50K, which is 31 miles in American, but I think it sounds more badass if you go with the higher number. So it's a 50K. In any case, the most I'd run in the past few years was probably closer to 12K. I ran a marathon once, and although it felt pretty recent, I now realized it was nine years ago.

I'm not what you'd call a "runner." I prefer it to getting fat, but not by a lot. Every once in a while, Jayson and Nick would talk me into a Saturday morning trail run, but I went along because I like them, not running, plus they went to the good pho place on Federal Boulevard on the way home after the trail run, and I love the Vietnamese coffee there. I had run a few times a week through the summer, but hardly ever had the attention span to go more than five miles. So this ultramarathon would be a pretty big stretch.

I had basically been circling the ultramarathon drain for a couple months, getting a little more curious as Jayson's training started to ramp up and mine didn't. I didn't have time for the runs, with a bike tour in Norway knocking out the first two weeks of July and a backpacking trip taking up nine days of August, plus all the other traveling I do. I had lots of other excuses.

But I had purchased two copies of Bryon Powell's *Relentless Forward Progress: A Guide to Running Ultramarathons*, and given one to Jayson, and kept one. With no ultra on the horizon, I had only flipped through it, searching for the word "walk." There it is, Page 106. Has its own section: "Walking, Your New Best Friend."

I met Bryon once at a happy hour thing. Seemed like a good guy. No way he'd bullshit me. If he says walking is a part of ultrarunning, I can be an ultrarunner.

I started running more. I got a vest: the Ultimate Direction SJ UltraVest 2.0, designed with input from Scott Jurek. Room for water and snacks, and not much more. I discovered with full water bottles, it tempered my stride down even further as I tried to minimize bouncing of the bottles.

The book said to try to eat 250 to 400 calories per hour when you were running long distances. This, I could get used to. I bought bags of Kettle Chips, dates, and electrolyte drinks, and stashed them in my van and parked it at Green Mountain just outside Denver, then ran 7.5-mile loops, returning to the van to refill my bottles and my belly after each lap. Snacks! I even started to eat what I normally referred to as Space Food, the semi-tasty gels and energy globules I thought only triathletes, road cyclists and other people trying to do shit fast ate. I shortened the name of my Ultimate Direction SJ UltraVest 2.0 to "The Suffer Vest."

I ran 19 miles, walking the hills, keeping a 13-minute-mile pace. OK, that's close to 31 miles. The next week,

I tried to run 22.5 miles. By the time I started my third lap, it was 80 degrees, and there was no shade. My legs hurt, the muscles holding that I've-been-standing-all-day fatigue. First my right shin hurt for a mile, then my left arch. Then my right Achilles tendon hurt for a couple miles, then it went away. I assumed this is how it went with these types of things, and that I would know when something hurt enough to be serious. I kept up a 13-minute-per-mile pace, running all the hills this time.

Some people temper the misery of long runs with music. I tried it once a long time ago, training for that marathon, and found it only helped a tiny bit, and kind of made me hate all the songs I listened to on my 4-hour training run. So I don't run with headphones, which is kind of boring, but I think I prefer a more pure kind of suffering. Plus I have this secret weapon.

At my pace, the sound of my short almost-shuffling strides and the water sloshing in the bottles in The Suffer Vest matches the exact rhythm of the first track on the Beastie Boys' *Licensed To Ill* album, "Rhymin and Stealin," specifically the chorus in which they repeat the phrase "Ali Baba and the Forty Thieves" eight times, starting with a whisper and crescendoing into their classic nasally yelling.

I own five Beastie Boys albums, and Licensed to Ill is my fifth favorite of them, if I'm honest about it. They're not even close to my favorite Golden Age hip hop group, but I love their music despite the fact that they basically freestyled their way through eight studio albums without once making a song that really said anything. But the line from this song popped into my head when I was running one day, and now I can't get it out. I just go with it. Ali Baba and the Forty Thieves. Ali Baba and the Forty Thieves. Why are they even saying that? Why is it the one line of the song they choose to repeat eight times? Why am I running for five hours with two water bottles strapped to my chest? Should I call this thing "The Shuffler Vest" instead? Whatever. Ali Baba and the Forty Thieves.

--

I finished 22.5 miles without walking. I didn't break anything. I had some chafing, and felt like a group of kids had been hitting me with sticks all morning while I stood in a sauna, but I could still stand up. Maybe I would be able to pee again by the end of the day? When I got home, I texted ultrarunner Luke Nelson.

Brendan to Luke: Dude I signed up for a 50K. Could you tell me the difference between ultrarunning and ultrashuffling? I am going to ultrashuffle, I think.

Luke to Brendan: Actually, the difference is only the mindset. In all reality, the pacing is the same, but if you feel like you are ultrarunning—generally a more positive, glass-half-full attitude—then you will be happier during the journey. Ultra shuffling is more commonly associated with suffering, dread, and despair (glass half empty). Finish time will likely be the same regardless of style. I would recommend ultrarunning.

The morning of the race, Hilary and I walked to the start/finish area with camp chairs, a cooler full of drinks, a bag of food, and sat shivering in not enough warm clothing through the start of Jayson's 50-mile race, then waited an hour for the start of the 50K.

My friend Syd, who has run half a dozen New York Marathons and more than 20 half marathons despite claiming that he's only enjoyed about 15 total minutes of his running career, showed up with a 64-square-foot tent and about 640 square feet of enthusiasm.

I swore I was going to walk the first two minutes, just to prevent getting swept up in the adrenaline and running too fast and wasting all my energy in the first couple miles. But then everyone started jogging so I started jogging too. It took a few miles for everyone to spread out so I could have some trail to myself. Finally, about Mile 4, the Shuffler Vest started bouncing in time with the Beastie Boys and I settled in. Then I got to the first aid station.

I am not a runner, but aid stations may make me an ultrarunner. The course was a 12.5-mile loop, and had three aid stations. I stopped to find tables laid out with peanut butter and jelly sandwiches, bean burritos, pickles, M&M's, Peanut M&M's, Skittles, Chips Ahoy!, Oreos, vanilla wafers, electrolyte drinks, and nice people handing me all of these things and refilling my water bottles. This was not a race—this was a buffet. And all you had to do was run three or four miles in between snacks! It was perfect. Feel guilty about eating a row of Oreos sitting at home watching Netflix? Don't. Sign up for an ultramarathon and watch the guilt melt away with the miles. Here, have another cookie.

--

I ran the first lap a little fast, then finished the second lap feeling pretty good. I passed a few people on the course, and they got ahead of me again when I took long breaks back in our tent. I tried to run everything that wasn't a significant uphill, and succeeded.
I carefully ate Space Food every half hour, and cookies at every aid station, making sure to fill a water bottle with electrolyte drink and salt each time. I knew it could all change in a matter of seconds, and I could go from feeling OK to feeling like garbage at any point if I wasn't careful, especially with the 85-degree heat and all the fluids I was sweating out.

At mile 26, I took my first step away from the aid station and felt a sharp pain in the side of my right knee. It hurt to jog. Holy shit it hurt to walk. I tried a slow lunge forward, then tried pulling my foot up behind my hamstring to stretch it out. No relief. I limped forward, still trying to take steps, hobbling away from the aid station. This was not one of those little aches and pains; this was an injury, wasn't it? Two hundred feet from the aid station, I halfway turned on the trail. Maybe I should go back. Call it a day. This was real pain. And this is what happens when you do something dumb, like trying to run an ultramarathon more or less off the couch.

What happens if I quit here? Do they send someone to pick me up? Do we call my girlfriend to come and get me? I can't even remember her phone number. I don't want to put people out. The logistics seem too complicated. I turned back on the trail and kept walking forward. I'll just walk the last five miles. Worst case, that will take an hour and a half or two hours. As long as the pain doesn't get any worse.

After a hundred steps or so, the trail started a small climb. I jogged a few steps. Hm. IT band? I stopped and dug my fingers into the side of my thigh, pushing hard and rubbing up and down. Then the heel of my hand. I took a step. That felt a little better, didn't it? I walked, then started jogging again. The trail turned downhill. I jogged, sharp pain, stopped, walked. No downhills.

I walked the flats and uphills most of the next mile and a half, then jogged the last half mile to the final aid station, 3.2 miles from the finish. I massaged my IT band, or where I thought it was, as hard as I could, then started running the last section. I felt OK.
I shuffle-ran the last three miles through the forest, figuring I'd kick it in and try to actually look like I was running for the last 500 feet or so to the finish line. It was OK, my knee was going to make it. No telling what would happen when I sat down for a few minutes after the race, but for now, it seemed like it wasn't serious.

Hilary jumped up from her seat about 400 feet from the finish and jogged in next to the trail as I picked up the pace a little bit—no sense sprinting, I figured. I was going to come in under seven hours, and I didn't really care about shaving off a few seconds at the end. Plus I wasn't too confident that I wouldn't come apart like Herbie the Love Bug if I pushed too hard.

Jayson finished his third lap, 37.5 miles, in high spirits, and Nick grabbed a Pacer bib and one of my water bottles to run the last 12.5 miles with him. We all waited as it got late, and the sun went down, and the trail got darker and darker. Finally, just after the 13-hour mark, Jayson and Nick popped over the last hill, running. They had walked most of the final lap, Jayson's IT band also revolting, as well as his digestive system. Almost exactly a decade earlier, Jayson had finished a marathon despite being what his physician described as "a little heavy." And now here he was, 70 pounds lighter, hobbling into the finish. My race number, 215, was donut-eating Jayson's weight in 2005.

Thirty-one miles was enough for me, I figured, seeing what kind of shape Jayson was in at the finish, considering how much he trained. We got a photo with our finisher medals and drove into Denver to eat victory pizza.

I slept ten hours and woke up the next morning a little stiff, but no permanent injuries. That afternoon, I started googling 50-mile races. I still wouldn't say I'm a runner, but I might be an ultrarunner. I mean, I don't love running, but I love cookies. And that might be a good enough reason.

3

THE ICE AGE TRAIL 50

Shortly after running the Bear Chase Trail Race 50K, Jayson and I started talking about running a race together. I can't remember if we had specifically said, "Let's work our way up to a 100-mile race" or not, but I think that was the idea, whether anyone said it out loud or not. Jayson had finished a 50-mile race for his first ultramarathon (although I'm not sure he'd recommend doing that as a first ultra distance), and I was curious. We decided on the Ice Age Trail 50 in southern Wisconsin in 2016, an important step, because who knew if I could handle that many miles in one day?

--

I guess my theory about ultramarathons is that everyone who's ever heard of them has two immediate questions: 1) Why the hell would you do something like that? and 2) I wonder if I could run that far?

How you answer those two questions, in your head, or out loud, dictates whether or not you actually end up finding yourself in an actual ultramarathon.

As for Question 1, I know why people do really painful

things like ultramarathons, mountaineering, and waiting in line for hours to see concerts: In some trick of psychology, you convince yourself the pain will be worth it. And afterward, most of the time, you believe it was worth it.

I signed myself up for the Ice Age Trail 50 last December, wondering if I could run 50 miles of rolling hills on trails through the Kettle Moraine State Forest in Wisconsin in a single day. Then I showed up to the starting line last Saturday under grey skies and 40-degree temps, no less sure I could do it than the day I signed up for the race.

Not content to only put myself through this much pain, I signed my friend Jayson up for the race as well, and we decided that we had two goals: Finish in time to get an Ice Age Trail 50 belt buckle, and be smiling at the end of it.

It was cold at the start line, at 6 a.m., and the 370 other 50-mile runners gathered in a loose mass around the start/finish line, most of us quite ordinary people with a variety of reasons to spend 9 or 10-plus straight hours on the move over a rough trail. Or trying until we broke ourselves, I guess. Then there were a handful of people I would call "real runners," the badasses who would maintain 8- or 9-minute miles throughout the entire race and finish in six or seven hours.

By Mile 2, the outside of my left foot started hurting, and I figured it would go away sometime, and the pain would move elsewhere, like it usually did during our training runs. Your body parts just take turns hurting, in my experience, and hopefully none of the pains you feel are actual injuries—although after running 20 miles or so, you have enough endorphins pumping through your body that you sometimes won't know if something actually broke until the next day or the day after that. At the second aid station—Mile 9—we ditched our light jackets, refilled our water bottles, and kept running, spirits high. We still felt good at the aid station at Mile 17.3 where our friends and family members met us with food and electrolyte drinks. At Mile 20, I began to feel fatigue in my legs, sort of like that feeling you get if you stand on your feet all day waiting tables or bartending, but in this case you keep running and walking, relentlessly, and you know the pain is not going to go away unless you stop moving. At Mile 26.2, I sat down for a couple minutes while filling water bottles and eating potato chips. We were over halfway through the 50 miles, but I felt not even the slightest inkling that we had it in the bag.

We leapfrogged a few of the same people throughout the race—they were good at moving through the aid stations quickly and we were not. I got distracted by Chips Ahoy and Oreos at every aid station, giving myself permission to eat as much crap as I wanted to, whether I needed it for calories or just emotional reasons.

We hoped to finish anytime before 6 p.m., just under the 12-hour cutoff. As the first "fast guy" passed us going the other direction, way ahead of our pace, I remembered something I'd read on the race website:

"The awards ceremony is at 3 p.m.," I said to Jayson, and we both laughed, knowing we'd still have 10 miles left to run at that point.

Around Mile 30, Jayson and I basically stopped talking to each other, the only sounds escaping our mouths involuntary grunts and sighs and the occasional "good job" as we passed a runner heading the other direction. At Mile 31.5, I was officially setting a personal record for The Longest Distance I've Ever Run in One Day.

Friends who had run ultras had told me before the race, "Everything changes after 30 miles." I kept thinking of that as the miles rolled by and I kept moving one foot in front of the other, occasionally kicking a rock or root and sending a shot of pain up my toes through my foot. And I kept thinking, "Nothing changes. It's just the same pain, gradually growing the more I keep moving."

I'm sure the scenery was wonderful. I commented on it at least twice to Jayson, and at one point he said, "I'm about to do a Cowardly Lion from *The Wizard of Oz*— 'I'm feeling tired. I think I might just lay down here for a nap.'" But most of it was just a blur of green, a moving meditation: focus on moving, ignore the aches and constant pain, ignore your watch, if it hurts to walk, you might as well run.

At 41.3 miles, we stopped at aid station #10 to see our family and friends, split a cinnamon roll with frosting, changed socks for nothing more than a morale boost, and ran back into the woods to finish the remaining miles. At the aid station at 43.5 miles, I heard a volunteer yell, "Does anyone else need a ride?" as a Subaru station wagon pulled up to take an injured runner to the finish. Temptation comes in many forms. I ate another Oreo and shuffled off down the trail behind Jayson.

Around mile 44.5, we passed a handmade sign that said, "If you feel good during an ultra, don't worry, it will pass."

Fifty miles. Could I run that far? I'm not sure where this idea came from. In mountaineering, you often have to get up to the top and back down if you want to survive, so that pushes you. But in ultrarunning, most of the time, you're not going to die—you can pretty much quit anytime you see that table full of cookies and ask someone to call you a ride.

I'm not saying either one is more hardcore, but having done some extremely long days in the mountains, I know how much those can hurt. While I kept shuffling through those last miles in the Ice Age Trail 50, I thought back to the time my friend Chris and I climbed the Grand Teton in a day a few years ago, and how tired I was on the descent that I almost fell asleep with my legs sticking across the trail in Garnet Canyon. This ultramarathon was for sure the most pain I'd ever been in for this long—a new frontier of fatigue. But there were cookies every few miles.

At mile 48.5, we passed the final aid station. As we jogged onto the gentle Nordic ski trail, I looked at my watch. Almost an hour to cover 1.5 miles. Plenty of time. I said to Jayson, "We'd have to massively fuck this up to not get belt buckles at this point."

"I would throw you over my shoulder and carry you," he said.

"I would actually be up for that right now, to be honest with you."

With 200 yards to go, we could hear the cheers of people at the finish line. At 50 yards, we saw our friends and family yelling just in front of the finish. Jayson started yelling and whooping in joy, and I felt more relief than joy, and just tried to keep my back straight and arms up so it didn't look like I was going to die before I crossed the finish.

As we crossed under the arch at the finish line, I had the answer to my question, that I could run 50 miles in one day. We were near the back of the pack, and as people crossed the finish line behind us, the cheers from the crowd got louder. The race, at least the dramatic competitive part we mythologize in most of the things we call "sports," is long over at that point. But I think what we're cheering for is something else: normal people who aren't there to necessarily race anyone besides the lesser person they might be if they didn't try to run a really long ways for no good reason.

We gathered our stuff and hobbled across the parking lot to leave, and as the crowd around the finish line went from cheering loudly to going bananas, I realized we were missing a moment: a runner was crossing the finish line at 11:59:13, the final person to finish before the 12-hour cutoff.

Maybe in a couple weeks, I'll start wondering if I can run 100 miles. After my foot stops hurting. If they have Oreos at the aid stations.

4

HAPPINESS IS YOUR BACKYARD TRAIL

In 10-plus years of writing a weekly blog, I am still never sure if anyone's reading what I'm writing (partly because I shut off the comments in 2016). Occasionally I get emails from readers and friends or meet someone in person and they'll mention a specific piece I wrote. This one always makes me think of the guy (who I won't name) who came up to me at a book signing event at the Denver REI store and we chatted a few minutes about how much he also loved Green Mountain. And then he explained he loved my stuff but had never supported me on Patreon because at the time he'd heard about it, he was unemployed. But to make up for that, he said, here's this—and he slapped a fifty-dollar bill in my hand.

--

I plodded my way up the Hayden Trail, headed up toward my fifth "summit" of the day as the sun coasted downward. I had eaten my last Clif Shot a while ago, and had drunk my last water with it. Most of the mountain bikers and hikers had gone home for the day, and I was clocking my fifth hour running around Green Mountain, attempting a contrived trail run in which I ran down every trail leading from the summit and then back up. I had miscalculated the distance, elevation gain, and food and water needed (by not trying to calculate it at all and just guessing). I was having a bit of an adventure, a little over 11 miles from my house, which I could theoretically see from the top of Green Mountain.

Green Mountain is nothing special by Colorado standards: a 6,854-foot mesa at the edge of the Denver suburbs, rising about 800 feet above the roads that border it, two of which are freeways. Calling it a mountain is a bit comical when you look at the range of peaks that rise literally right behind it (on a clear day, you can see three 14,000-foot peaks from the summit). It's not even the most famous "Green Mountain" in the Front Range—Boulder's Green Mountain holds the famous Flatirons on its east face, and Chautauqua Park below those. The Green Mountain I run on is a big hill, lacking the forested trails and rocky crags of its taller, steeper neighbors.

But I love that goddamn big hill with no trees, sitting in front of the "real" mountains. It has 17.5 miles of trails, and I've run, walked, and mountain biked at least a thousand miles on those trails. None of them lead to a breathtaking waterfall or across a creek or a river. People don't even take selfies on the summit—it's kind of just a flat area that sometimes has a cairn on it. But like an old loyal dog or a reliable but scratched-up old bicycle, it's mine. Or rather, it's ours—myself and the dozens of people whose cars fill the Green Mountain parking lots on weekends and after work on weekdays.

For every Instagram-worthy, magazine-cover-headline-inspiring, do-this-before-you-die trail, there are thousands of miles of unsung (or less-sung) trails like those. When people ask, "What's your favorite trail?" we tell them some trail we've been on once or twice in our lives, instead of the one we could walk blindfolded. And we keep going back to our backyard trails not because of one or two unforgettable experiences, but because of dozens of good experiences.

Green Mountain's trails are usually the first ones to dry out in the spring or after a snowstorm, and plenty of people know it. I'm used to sharing it with a few dozen hikers, runners, bikers, and dogs on weekends, but also watching hundreds of cars drive past it to head up I-70 to go skiing for the day. Lots of days it's what you might call "crowded," but some days, you get the place to yourself for a few minutes—near sunrise, when you might surprise a rattlesnake or two, or near sunset, when you might hear the haunting party howls of a pack of coyotes somewhere nearby.

Hell, you know what, my favorite trail is not Angel's Landing in Zion National Park, or the Glacier Gorge Trail in Rocky Mountain National Park, or the Hardergrat in Switzerland. It's a few miles of trails in William Frederick Hayden Park on Green Mountain 25 minutes from my house, which I talk about like someone talks about an old car and all its quirks: there's no shade in the summer, it doesn't get very high, the trails aren't technical at all, sometimes on a busy Saturday you have to step off the trail 30 or 40 times to let people pass, it gets windy up on the top, there are snakes in the summertime, I've been up there so many times it kind of feels like going to the gym, there's nowhere to hide if you have to unexpectedly use the bathroom … but it's my favorite. You know, this old thing? It's no John Muir Trail, but I guess it's pretty OK.

Last Sunday, as the sun started to dip below the mountains to the west, I jogged off the top of Green Mountain to head down to my car to finally get some food and water. I saw five people total in the last mile of fire road to the parking lot, downright peaceful for a busy Sunday. Peaceful enough that a deer stood in the middle of the fire road, looking up at me until I got about 80 feet from it and it bounded into the next gully—where 20 of its friends waited, all staring at me in the last minutes of golden sunlight.

OK, yeah, this is my favorite trail.

5

THE RUN RABBIT RUN 100

Early on in my career writing for Adventure Journal, *I emailed Steve Casimiro, the founder and editor, and mentioned a story idea I'd happened upon, about a race somewhere. Steve replied to my email with a succinct, "We don't cover anything with a stopwatch." Fast-forward a few years and Steve had started a beautiful* Adventure Journal *quarterly print publication, and asked if I had anything I was interested in writing about. I said something like "how about ultrarunning," hoping he was no longer sticking to the no-stopwatch rule. He wasn't, and this piece appeared in* Adventure Journal 08, *with the title "Forward On The Fumes of Ambition." We made a film about this race, called "How to Run 100 Miles," but this essay is the only thing I've ever written about it. It was my first 100-mile race.*

--

From about mile 74 of the Run Rabbit Run 100 onward, I basically turned into a cranky, sullen two-year-old: I didn't talk much, I walked a lot, I kept stopping to use the bathroom or eat more snacks or sit in a camp chair at aid stations way too long, and my pace slowed to just under 23 minutes per mile. Brody, my pacer, started became a babysitter tasked more with my survival than a performance metric.

What do you want to eat? Brody asked.

I'm not hungry, I muttered.

You have to eat something. You need calories.

I'm good. I'm not hungry.

You have to eat. What sounds good?

Nothing.

Peanut butter and jelly sandwiches? Pancakes?

Pancakes.

OK, pancakes.

Everything went this way. How do your feet feel? They're fine. How about we take your shoes off and check? No. Sorry, I'm taking your shoes off and wiping your feet down, and we're changing your socks. OK.

Are you ready to go? I guess so. Are your water bottles full? Yes. You have food? Yes.

And then I'd ask myself one question: Wouldn't it be nice to just stop right now, instead of going all the way to Mile 102.9? This, of course, is a perfectly rational thought, because running 100 miles all at once is one of the dumbest things you can do for fun.

Like anything worth doing, I suppose, running long distances is about 90 percent tedious bullshit and 10 percent wonderful. Maybe more or less, depending on your outlook—my girlfriend, for example, loves it. But I don't. When it comes up in conversation that I'm training for another ultramarathon, people say, "I could never do that—I hate running." I just kind of shrug and say, "I do too."

But, like someone who's spending another weekend grouting shower tile or putting up drywall and wondering what the hell they were thinking when they bought a house that needed a little work, there you are. So I fill up some water bottles, grab some space-food energy gels and cubes and stuff them into a running vest, put lubricant on my upper thighs and chest, and tell myself: normal people do this. This is normal.

And then I go run on trails for 20 or 25 miles, watching for rocks and tree roots, noticing the difference in morale when I'm running uphill vs. running downhill, listening to nothing but my wheezing breath and the various aches and pains in my feet, ankles, knees, and hips.

I am not a gazelle, like those famous runners you've seen on magazine covers. I am working. I have at points done real work in my life, digging holes, standing on assembly lines getting too many parts per minute delivered to me on conveyor belts, shoveling, swinging hammers, carrying heavy loads. All that stuff either a) prepared me for running long distances or b) was way smarter because I was getting paid for it, unlike running.

But everyone understands running, on some level. It's not like climbing. If you're on an airplane and you end up revealing to your seatmate that you're a climber, and they have no experience with it, they will ask you if you do things like that guy who climbed El Capitan without a rope, or if you've climbed Everest. Which makes sense, because most of the world's population has never tied into a rope and climbed up something for fun.

But everyone gets running, whether they've run a 10K in the past year, or just remember running as a kid. When you're an adult, though, people will give you way more reasons to not run than to run, and all those reasons are true: it's boring, it hurts, probably during 10 to 100 percent of your runs you wonder if, when, and where you're going to have to poop, and it's just not that fun.

Well, no offense to your most recent romantic relationship, but what percent of that is actual fun? Probably not 100 percent, I'm guessing. You probably don't even like it, or parts of it, at times. But you love it. You love that other person, even though they're not perfect and you're not perfect, and maybe a little annoying at times, if you're completely honest. That's how I feel about running: I don't like it all the time, but I love it.

--

In 2010, long before I started running long distances, I interviewed alpinist and writer Kelly Cordes about the idea of being "hardcore." I listed off a few things Kelly had done, big high-altitude mountaineering expeditions where he and his partner ran out of food and water and barely survived, stumbling back into their basecamp totally strung out (this happened several times). I said, Kelly, you're pretty hardcore, don't you think?

He humbly replied that no, no, he wasn't that hardcore (which is incorrect), but do you know who was, he said? Ultrarunners. In climbing, he said, it's easy to get yourself into a situation where you have no choice but to keep moving—because if you don't, you'll die. But in an ultramarathon, it's different.

"I look at my ultramarathoner friends—OK, so they're running like 100 miles, voluntarily," Kelly said. "So once you start hurting halfway through, and everybody hurts, there's no way anyone feels good for 100 miles – why not just quit? You know, seriously. Why not just call it good at the aid station, sit down, snap your fingers and call for a beer and a bag of chips and say, 'I'm done, my legs are tired.' You know, that will to keep going when you have no reason to, that, in a sense, that's actually way hardcore. I think in some ways way more hardcore than situations where you really don't have a choice but to continue."

I heard Kelly, and that idea burrowed into my subconscious, waiting for the right conditions to hatch. I was curious about these people who ran 50 or 100 miles, and maybe, just a little bit, wondered if I could become one of them. But I considered myself a climber, not a runner.

Two years later, I was at the base of the second pitch of the Kor-Ingalls route on Castleton Tower with my friend Chris, letting a pair of climbers pass us after rockfall had cut our rope in three places. The young man leading the pitch fell from about 25 feet above me, clipped his foot on something, and landed face-first on the belay ledge next to us. He had a seizure, and we tied him into our anchor and began to initiate a rescue. The slap of skin and bones on rock was sickening and terrifying—probably exactly what would have happened if someone fell off the roof of a house and landed on a sidewalk. After six hours and a helicopter rescue, the young man got to a hospital and eventually was fine. But something had shifted for me.

I kept climbing for another year, with less of the fervor I'd had for it for the previous six years. In 2013, staring up at the endless splitter crack on Lunar Ecstasy in Zion National Park, I realized I was feeling more dread than excitement for climbing. So I took a break. I got back into skiing, did a little mountain biking, some bikepacking, and almost never tied into a rope.

In 2015, Kelly Cordes's idea broke open in my brain: I signed up for my first ultramarathon, with only 23 days to train to run 31 miles. I barely finished, thanks to an IT band that felt like someone was poking my leg with a cattle prod for a couple miles. I walked probably five or six miles of the course, and definitely didn't feel like a natural at it: I finished 78th, exactly three hours after the first runner had crossed the finish line.

But fuck me, I loved it. I had kept moving, on trails, in nature, for almost seven straight hours. It was the same joy I'd felt hiking and running from rim to rim in the Grand Canyon, and climbing the Grand Teton in a day, only it was made a little more sane by having aid stations every few miles, staffed with people whose job was to help you keep going. It was all the pain and suffering of mountaineering without the risk of dying in an accident. I mean sure, maybe I felt like I was going to die, but I probably wasn't really in danger. Give me the word for the joy of moving all day just because you still can, and I'll tell you, this is the definition of it. A sick joy, but joy.

Eight months later, I signed up for a 50-mile race, hit rock bottom at about mile 42, and dragged my ass through the final eight miles to cross the finish line a half-hour before the cutoff. Which was good enough for me—it was more about whether I could actually finish a 50-mile race, not how fast I could do it.

As I walked through the parking lot with my friends and family after the race, I heard a tremendous roar come up from the crowd at the finish line. I paused for a second, wondering what happened, and realized: the clock was ticking down, and the final runner had come through, 47 seconds before the cutoff. It was the running version of a team hitting a buzzer-beating basket to win the game—except the cheers weren't for the winner, they were for last place. People cheered for the runner's spirit, not her mastery of the sport. How could I not love this? Winning something is admirable, but rare. Trying fucking hard, no matter who you are or how long it takes you, is what puts a lump in my throat.

I checked off one more 50-mile race, slow but steady, and then I started to train for my first 100-mile race, ruining all my weekends for six months leading up to race day by spending them not staying up late and going on dates with my girlfriend, but running 18 to 50 miles on Saturday and/or Sunday and being almost completely immobile when I got home. It became a part-time job, and everyone was ready for it to be over by the time race day rolled around.

--

As far as I know, there's no ultrarunning quote analogous to Sir Edmund Hillary's "Because it's there." But during 23-mile training runs, 50-mile races, and a 102.9-mile race, I've had some of the most hope-deprived moments of my adult life. Climbing, for me, was always worth the risk-, the rockfall, the runouts, the tiny missteps and plain bad luck that have killed so many people in the mountains. And then one day it wasn't worth it to me. But I still wanted, in some way, to see what I was made of.

And running long distances—"long" being completely subjective—will grind you down, just like Kelly Cordes said. It beats you until you have nothing left besides some half-notion that you aren't a quitter, and you keep moving forward on the fumes of the ambition you had when you signed up for the race nine months ago, or the hopes of your friends and family who have shown up to support you.

I crossed the finish line of the Run Rabbit Run 100 at mile 102.9 with only 32 minutes to spare, clocking 35.5 continuous hours of motion. Someone handed me a belt buckle, and six months of hard work was over— although if I were to be honest, it was more like two years, from the start of my first ultramarathon.

Four months later, I'm still putting on that ridiculous running vest with all my water and space-age foods in it, heading up to the foothills, and spending hours tromping around on trails, enjoying a few minutes of it here and there, when the evening sun hits the trees just right or a herd of elk pass by. But mostly I just can't stop myself right now.

I don't know if that makes me a runner. I still don't know if I even like running. Maybe I just love trying hard.

6

THE RIM-TO-RIM-TO-RIM: A TRAIL DIARY

After the Run Rabbit Run 100, I didn't know if I'd ever run another 100-mile race, but I knew I wanted to keep trail running. My friend Forest Woodward talked me into a 50-mile race in North Carolina in February 2018, which was my third 50-mile race. Then I happened to be in Flagstaff in April, with a few days conveniently between commitments, and I thought I might as well give the Grand Canyon Rim-to-Rim-to-Rim a shot. I asked my friend Mitsu Iwasaki if he'd like to come down from Portland to join, and he made a very quick trip to do it. It had been warm for the past couple weeks, and I don't do particularly well in the heat. I also was wary of the R2R2R being a bit crowded, spring and fall being the big seasons for people from all over the world attempting it. But the forecast switched to mercifully cool and, less mercifully, extremely windy. It ended up being an interesting day.

--

4:35 a.m.:
The wind blows across the South Rim of the Grand Canyon, 20 mph constant. Mitsu and I hurriedly grab hats and gloves, pull on running vests and slam car doors in the dark in front of the Bright Angel Lodge. It's 45 degrees as we quickly walk a couple hundred feet to the Bright Angel trailhead, where the lights of the South Rim disappear and a big black hole eats up the horizon.

My layering strategy—a pair of running shorts and a hooded wind jacket over a thin long-sleeve synthetic top—is basically me betting that today's forecasted winds will disappear once we step below the rim. A hundred steps down the trail, it's quiet again, and I'm relieved to cross "hypothermia" off my list of Things That Could Go Wrong During My Rim-to-Rim-to-Rim Run."

Items still remaining on that list:
- Blisters
- Chafing
- Dehydration
- Shitting my pants
- Spraining or breaking an ankle or other body part crucial to locomotion
- Tripping and falling off an exposed section of trail
- Finishing way too late to get to the Cornish Pasty place in Flagstaff
- Realizing that my entire life up until this point has been a lie
- Discovering that I'm not tough enough to do this after all

- Running out of food

Just kidding. I have literally never run out of food in the backcountry. I have 4,380 calories stuffed in my running vest:

- 10 single-serving packets of Skratch Labs Sport Hydration Drink Mix (800 calories)
- 3 small bags crushed Kettle Chips (660 calories)
- 8 chocolate Clif Shots (880 calories)
- 2 Vega One bars (540 calories)
- 2 Panda Raspberry Licorice bars (200 calories)
- 3 packages Black Cherry Clif Shot Bloks (600 calories)
- 5 Cinnamon Honey Stinger waffles (700 calories)

We run by headlamp, the canyon dark beyond our personal LED-lit bubbles. The stair-stepped trail makes it hard to establish a stride, so I intermittently walk and jog. After 15 minutes, I remove my wind layer.

5:57 a.m.:
The canyon starts to light up in the pre-dawn minutes, and a few hundred feet above Indian Garden, we run into the first backpackers hiking up and out of the canyon. I was worried about being quiet as we ran past the campground so we didn't wake anyone, but it looks like almost everyone is packed up already.
Mitsu stops at the restroom and I fill up my water bottles while I wait. Almost five miles down so far. We mostly run the rest of the descent to the Colorado River and meet more hikers on their way up from Phantom Ranch. We cross the river on the silver bridge, and pass

Phantom Ranch at Mile 10ish at 7:15 a.m.

8:15 a.m.:
Around Mile 15, Mitsu's strained something-or-other has grown increasingly painful, and he decides to turn back. We make plans to meet back at Phantom Ranch when I come back through in a few hours. I tell him I'll hustle so he won't have to wait too long, and also so I can maybe get a coffee before the canteen closes for dinner. For a second, I consider bailing with him, because drinking lemonade at Phantom Ranch sounds way more fun than finishing the 5,800-foot climb up to the North Rim.

Here's the great thing about the Rim-to-Rim-to-Rim: it's basically a semi-supported ultramarathon. There are water spigots in six places along the trail, and in season, seven others. You do have to carry all your own food (unless you time it right and can buy candy bars from the canteen at Phantom Ranch). There are no aid stations, no volunteers sweeping the course, almost no meeting places for anyone to "crew" you, and hopefully not that many other people. And if you snap your ankle, it'll probably be a long time before you get rescued. I brought a space blanket and some water treatment tablets. My mother told me to be careful, so I did that too, for her, and also to avoid being a pain in the ass for the park service.

9:20 a.m.:
I reach Manzanita, mile 17.5, after a bunch of power-hiking and jogging. The water, which has been turned off for a few months, has been temporarily and fortuitously turned on, so I fill my bottles. The wind is blowing steady and gusting up to about 30 mph, so I

make a vow to only pee in pit toilets the rest of the day, in order to minimize stops and also to minimize accidentally spraying myself with my own urine. Not that there's anything wrong with that. I've just had some windy restroom adventures out there and realized that peeing on my own face wasn't really my thing.

A Brief History of the Rim-to-Rim-to-Rim:

- 13.799 ± 0.021 billion years ago: Big Bang happens
- 5-6 million years ago: Grand Canyon is formed
- Early 1900s: The Cameron Trail, which was originally built to Indian Garden by the Havasupai tribe and will later be known as the Bright Angel Trail, completes its route from the South Rim all the way to the Colorado River.
- 1925: The South Kaibab Trail, another trail from the South Rim to the Colorado River, is completed.
- 1928: The North Kaibab Trail, connecting the North Rim to the Colorado River, is finished, completing a rim-to-rim route.
- Sometime after 1928: Somebody hikes the whole thing from rim to rim in a day
- Also sometime after 1928: Somebody hikes the whole thing from rim to rim to rim in a day
- 2016: Jim Walmsley sets the Fastest Known Time for a Rim-to-Rim-to-Rim run, 5 hours, 55 minutes, 20 seconds*
- 2017: Cat Bradley sets the women's FKT for the Rim-to-Rim-to-Rim: 7 hours, 52 minutes, 20 seconds*
- 2018: I decide to run the Rim-to-Rim-to-Rim*.

There are two different routes to do a Rim-to-Rim-to-Rim. The one that utilizes the South Kaibab Trail is 42 miles total, and is a little steeper on the South Rim side. The one that uses the Bright Angel Trail is 48 miles total, and is less steep on the South Rim side. You can imagine if you were trying to set a record, you'd do the 42-mile version. I was not setting a record, so I chose the 48-mile route.

11:29 a.m.:
After hiking nonstop up 3600 feet in 5.5 miles from the Manzanita rest area, I pop out on the North Rim to an empty North Kaibab Trailhead parking lot. I feel like pig vomit but at least the next 14 miles are all downhill. The wind continues to blast and I'm now at 8241 feet and getting chilled, so I quickly fill my water bottles, throw all my food wrappers in the trash can, and walk the first ½ mile of the trail while pouring crushed salt and pepper Kettle Chips into my mouth.

What's not really productive or nice to think about here is that if I were fast like Cat Bradley or Jim Walmsley, I'd be finished or nearly finished by now. Alas, I am not fast. Also, I like bread and sitting on my ass 40-50 hours a week for work. So here we are, headed back into the maw of the largest canyon in Coconino County, Arizona. My ears and nostrils are fully coated with blown dust. I run 90 percent of the next 5.5 miles back down to Manzanita.

12:57 p.m.:
I have crossed the 50 km mark, and I'm starting to think it will actually feel good to stop running downhill and start hiking uphill around mile 39. I stop at Manzanita,

where another guy is resting on his way up to the North Rim, and we chat a little bit but the wind is gusting up to 40 mph so I can barely hear anything he says. There used to be a basketball hoop here, right at this ranger residence a few thousand feet below the North Rim. A ranger told me once that they used to play full-on pickup games here, and every once in a while, the ball would bounce into the creek and float eight miles all the way down to Phantom Ranch, and basketball would be over until someone hiked the ball back up to Manzanita. They got rid of the hoop sometime in 2010 or 2011, regrettably.

2:12 p.m.:
I am officially eating shit. After moving as fast as I could for 9.5 hours, I hit the proverbial wall in The Box, the tight inner gorge of Vishnu Schist that winds along Bright Angel Creek for the final five miles to Phantom Ranch. This morning, The Box was almost completely shaded, and now it's not. I start giving myself any excuse to walk: too rocky, slightly uphill, too hot. When I see hikers, I jog, not wanting to give a bad name to my fellow dipshits who come down here in running shorts and funny-looking vests and try to cross Grand Canyon National Park twice in a day. At one point, I lean into a tiny bit of shade to try to check the GPS on my phone, a desperate move. I'm close to Phantom Ranch and all the Lemmy Lemonade I can drink, or at least all the Lemmy Lemonade I can buy with the $11 cash I have in my running vest.

2:46 p.m.:
I open the door of the Phantom Ranch canteen and see Mitsu at a table, the remnants of an Arnold Palmer in front of him. He asks if I want a coffee or lemonade,

and suddenly for about two seconds I feel like I might vomit. In a flash of bravery/stupidity, I say it would probably be best if we just keep moving. We get up and walk. Between Phantom Ranch and filling my water bottles at the horse corral next to the river, somehow 30 minutes go by.

As we walk across the silver bridge, I watch the blue-green water of the Colorado roll by 30 feet below my feet. I decide that the Rim-to-Rim-to-Rim is a hell of a great experience, but also far from the best way to see the Grand Canyon. I think about the backpacking trips I've done here and the monthlong raft trip, and watching the colors change, and this seems like trying to squeeze a marriage into a first date. But even if it's too fast, it's still pretty amazing.

I definitely have two huge blisters now, and some new pain in my heel that I hope isn't some sort of stress fracture. We keep hiking, and about a quarter-mile from Pipe Creek, a 3-foot long snake falls off the rock wall to our left and Mitsu barely avoids stepping on it as we both nearly piss our pants in simultaneous shock, and then we realize it's not a rattlesnake as it slithers off the trail. First time I've seen the old snake-falling-out-of-the-sky trick. Mitsu too.

5:40 p.m.:
We're only a few hundred feet from the 3-Mile Resthouse and I am pretty sure Mitsu has started hiking faster in an attempt to get us out of the canyon faster. I am filled with equal parts contempt and gratitude for this strategy but say nothing, choosing to instead think of something positive, like the fact that the next Clif Shot I eat might be the last one of the day, or maybe

even the month, or that maybe after we top out on the South Rim after another 2,100 vertical feet, I'll pull my head out of my ass and give up ultrarunning for something more enjoyable, like breaking rocks with a sledgehammer.

7:06 p.m.:
We arrive at the Bright Angel Trailhead. It's cold and windy. We get into the car, turn on the heat, drink canned coffee drinks, and drive straight to the Cornish Pasty place in Flagstaff.

7

A NEW YORK PIZZA MARATHON

One time during a race, I jogged a few miles with a younger guy who had discovered ultrarunning a year and a half prior, and had dived in headfirst, doing something like ten races in 14 months. His big goal, he said, was to run the Badwater 135. I asked him if he'd heard about that race in Dean Karnazes' book, Ultramarathon Man, *and he said yes, the Badwater was his favorite part of the book. I said that's cool, my favorite part of the book was the beginning, when he orders a pizza in the middle of a really long run and then eats the pizza while running, carrying the box in one hand and shoving slices into his mouth with the other hand. Anyway, nice guy, but he and I have different dreams.*

--

The concept was pretty simple, and potentially disgusting: Run a marathon, 26.2 miles, around New York City, and eat five slices of pizza—one slice approximately every five miles.

You might think this sounds like a terrible idea, and you'd probably be correct. Most sensible people don't like running long distances. Most sensible people who like pizza find it way more enjoyable if they don't have to run five miles while trying to digest it. Most sensible people wouldn't risk gastrointestinal distress in America's largest, and busiest, city, whose scarcity of public restrooms is so well-known that there are multiple websites and apps dedicated to finding places to pee. Obviously we are not sensible people. We are idiots.

We met in Bedford-Stuyvesant at 4 p.m. on Friday afternoon: swashbuckling adventure photographer Forest Woodward, filmmaker Sanjay Rawal (whose film *3100: Run and Become* is wonderful), and myself. Forest and I have both finished several ultramarathons, and Sanjay has run the Sri Chinmoy Six-Day Race, covering 240 miles. I'm not saying we're elite runners or anything; we just know how to stop and eat.

At the 1.5-mile mark in Brooklyn, we passed Junior's, and you know, the cheesecake is pretty legendary there, so we stopped and got a slice to split. And then ran across the Brooklyn Bridge and into Tribeca, where we grabbed our first slice at Dona Bella Pizza at Mile 4.0, ate it on the sidewalk outside, and then ran west to the Hudson River Greenway, a great place to avoid rush hour traffic for several miles. After 2 1/2 miles of bike path along the Hudson, we ducked back into the Theater District to get a coffee, take an emergency bathroom stop, and run through Times Square and then pick up our friend Carl at Columbus Circle.

We hadn't set out to link up the "best" five slices in New York—that would have been a lot of planning and logistics (I considered using a list I'd found in an Eater article). Easier plan: Run five miles, look around for a pizza spot, eat a slice. We figured we'd probably never be further than four or five blocks from a pizza joint the entire run, except when crossing bridges. Fortuitously, our route took us right past La Traviata at mile 10.9, a favorite dive my friend Syd introduced me to a few years ago. I was afraid I'd be unable to resist the eggplant slice, despite all my prior knowledge of running and digestion telling me eating a fifth of an eggplant was a bad idea. I was right.

In a pizza marathon, we learned, you cannot realistically expect to enjoy every slice of pizza. At best, you will like the taste of the first one, and maybe the second one. The third one, from Sliced by Harlem Pizza Co. near Columbia University at mile 15.8, really deserved a better audience than us. We took our third slices down with the enthusiasm of a pouting 4-year-old being held hostage at the dinner table by a plate of asparagus. Carl, a slice and 10 miles behind the rest of us, may have enjoyed the first bites of his—although our slices were a bit more spaced out than his.

We trudged south through Central Park, mostly still clocking sub-10-minute miles and also not shitting our pants, both proud achievements. We turned left out of the park at mile 20 and headed down 59th Street toward John & Tony's Pizza just before the Queensboro bridge. Sanjay opted for the no-cheese Sicilian slice, which we all agreed was probably a good idea. I let my cheese slice sit on the table for probably four minutes before I worked up the courage to pick it up and put it in my mouth.

We ran across the Queensboro Bridge in the dark, with cars zooming by in both directions. My right foot hurt, so did my right IT band, and I looked down at the apartment buildings on Roosevelt Island, their warm lamp light and television screens, probably all filled with people who were doing a better job relaxing than us. Our Friday night was contrived, foolish, and objectively pretty uncomfortable for many reasons, and there's a long list of more normal things we could be doing with our time (with a lot less sweating and chafing).

But I've always had more fun dreaming up things to do, making my own fun instead of waiting for something fun to be happening where I am. This, I would like to think, is the same spirit behind every adventure film festival, every new bikepacking route, and every original climbing linkup. I say even if you can't climb three classic 5.10 alpine routes in Rocky Mountain National Park in a day (I can't), you might be able to, for example, bicycle 25 miles between the three best taco joints where you live, or hike to the summit of two peaks in a day. You may have heard of the New York City Marathon—it's kind of a big deal. I've tried to sign up three different times and never gotten in. So we made our own.

At mile 26.7 (on Forest's Strava, because *mine said 25.3*), after 5 hours and 51 minutes (including sitting down to eat all the slices), we trudged into Paulie Gee's Slice Shop in Greenpoint, the only other must-eat-spot on our itinerary, and I performed the chewing equivalent of running a 45-minute mile. It was unfair to the legendary Paulie Gee's to eat there when we were so full of, and grossed out by, pizza. But I could tell it was good, in the way you might know a Bentley drives really nice even if you're just sitting in it without starting the engine.

NOTE: According to Strava, I burned 4,000 calories on our run. According to estimates of the calorie content of a typical plain New York slice (482 calories), I probably ate 2,500 calories, not including the fried eggplant on my Traviata slice. So it was still a net loss.

8

WHY FINISH LINES WILL GET YOU EVERY TIME

My friend Doug Mayer owns a trail running tour company called Run the Alps, and invited me to be a special guest on one of the trips in 2018. He also convinced me to arrive in France a few days early to hang out and take in the Ultra Trail du Mont Blanc scene. I was a hard sell at first, thinking I couldn't take even more time off work,, and then figured OK, sure. The first night in town, I happened to be walking by the finish just as some of the runners in the week's first event, the OCC, were crossing the finish line. I was immediately hooked, and then for the rest of the week, I couldn't get enough time hanging out at the finish area, as racers came through. Maybe I got a little emotional about the whole thing?

--

I didn't know why it happened. I was doing OK until the guy with the dog came through, and then, all of a sudden, I had a lump in my throat the size of a baseball.

I arrived in downtown Chamonix just in time for the finish of the OCC, the 55K trail ultramarathon preceding the Ultra Trail du Mont Blanc, which is basically the Super Bowl of ultrarunning. A friend was supposed to be finishing sometime in the next hour or two, so I figured I'd head to the finish and wait for him.

If you've never seen it, the last few hundred feet of the UTMB events course (including but not limited to the 55km OCC, the 101km CCC, and 170km UTMB) is pretty special: gates steer runners down a winding course through Chamonix, ending under a huge arch in front of the church at the Place du Triangle de l'Amitié. What makes it special are the spectators who line the final few hundred feet of the finish area, drumming on the boards attached to the gates every time a runner comes through to the finish. Friends, family, fans of running, people on their way home from the bar who have stopped to watch out of curiosity—everyone cheers and claps and pounds on the boards (even though the event emcees regularly ask spectators to please just clap instead).

It's also special because people are cheering, clapping, and drumming for runners regardless of their place in the race. The events of the UTMB are popular—like 1500 to 2300 runners in each event popular. So if you spend a half an hour at the finish line, you might see several dozen people come through.

I got sucked in. I didn't know anyone running besides the one person, but I went nuts just like everyone else for all the runners who ran past me through the finish arch. I pounded on the boards, I whooped, I clapped, I cheered, I shot iPhone videos of people I didn't know and would never meet as they ran past, and I didn't know why.

OCC runners jogged past, each one clad in different ultra vests and backpacks, each one a different story of how much the race challenged them. Some jogged past with relief on their faces, seeing the arch and an end to almost 10 hours of movement through the mountains; some smiled and screamed and high-fived the lines of spectators as they blew past; some twisted their mouths and gutted out the final hundred feet, digging deep.

Some runners grabbed their toddlers out of the crowd and ran through the finish; some ran the final dozen steps holding hands with their street-clothed spouses; some grabbed the hands of their young children who ran alongside them, obviously proud of Mom or Dad. I kept it together until a guy stopped 150 feet from the end and grabbed the leash of his dog, and then ran through the finish with the dog, who wagged his tail and gazed up adoringly as they finished the race together. I took a deep breath and smiled, trying to choke down the lump in my throat. Where did that come from?

My wife gets emotional every time she watches running, whether it's *Chariots of Fire*, the Olympics, or the finish line of a 10K race. I never really understood why until I started doing ultramarathons.

I noticed a couple things at my first 50-mile race: First, aside from the top, say, 15 or 20 percent of runners, it was full of what seemed like pretty regular people (including myself). We weren't super-athletes, just a bunch of normal people trying something a little harder (OK, way harder) than what's considered normal. Second, the loudest cheering at the finish line came for the person who got last place in the race—the final person who finished just a few minutes before the 12-hour cutoff time. This is apparently not uncommon.

In the competitive sports world I grew up in, which I assume is like most of America and the world, we cheered for winners. The losing team got polite applause, and so did everyone in second through eighth place in track and field. But certainly not the loudest cheers.

If you've ever run a marathon in a city, you've probably noticed that people come out to cheer. Not just for the first-place person—for everyone who passes by. Marathon spectators cheer, offer words of encouragement, and ring cowbells for anyone who's out there running. If you're running, this is fantastic. You could be an hour or two hours behind the person in first place, and total strangers are telling you you're doing a great job.

If you run through the finish of one of the UTMB races in Chamonix, you must feel like a superhero, with all the applause, drumming, and cheering. I can only speak for myself and the feeling I got from other spectators, but I don't think it's fake there—I think most of us are genuinely moved by watching runners giving it hell in the final stretch.

Running, unlike a lot of sports, is almost universal. Most of us have never (and may never) know what it's like to drain a three-point shot over someone to win a game, or catch a touchdown pass, or tear down an Alaskan spine on a snowboard. But everyone knows what it's like to run when you're tired, to dig deep, whether it's a mile or 100 miles. And when we see someone else doing it, trying hard, we're moved. And we cheer. We're not impressed with some athletic skill that we could never imagine mastering ourselves; we're impressed that they're out there, gritting their teeth through pain and pushing themselves to go further and be a little better. And whether they're in 10th place or 1500th place, we're inspired just a little bit. And occasionally, we get a little emotional about it. Which is a wonderful experience.

9

FEAR AND GROANING AT THE HELLBENDER 100

In 2020, I decided to try to look back on a decade of writing about "adventure," and pick 12 of my favorite adventures of the past 10 years. I wanted the adventures to be a mix of different types of trips and big days out, so I figured I could include one ultramarathon, but not more than that. But which one? It didn't take me long to decide on the Hellbender 100, which was one of the hardest days I've ever had in the mountains—scratch that, one of the hardest days I've had anywhere. I thought for a half-second, and only a half-second, about whether an organized race actually counted as an adventure. I looked up "adventure" in the dictionary and it said "an exciting or remarkable experience," so, *looks around* we're good here.

--

Somewhere around Mile 62 around 2:30 in the morning, I realized I hadn't seen another light in about an hour: no other runners, no houses, no car headlights, nothing besides the little headlamp bubble of light in front of me. I had kept my headlamp dimmed to conserve the battery, just chugging along through the forest, jogging with my trekking poles in my hands.

The entire trail had been covered in fallen leaves for miles, and it occurred to me a few times that I could be totally lost, but every time I started to worry, another little orange course marker flag would pop up. I was totally alone, and would be unless I sat down for an hour and waited for another runner to show up.

It was dead quiet, no wind, no sounds besides my feet shuffling through the wet leaves, and my breathing. If an animal had stepped on a stick 80 feet away, I would have heard it. I had been moving for 22 hours, and I felt OK, besides my soaking wet feet and the beginnings of fatigue that starts to set in when you've been going that long. I started thinking about the completely dark, dead quiet forest, and being totally alone.

For a half second, my brain flashed to an idea, completely out of nowhere: This was a horror movie scene, and a crazed killer with an axe or other implement of destruction would come rushing at me from the dark forest to the left or right, totally surprising me because my headlamp was so dim. Then, as quickly as the thought appeared, I said to myself, "What the fuck are you doing?" and pushed it out of my mind, choosing to focus on the joy of moving through the forest in solitude instead.

I never watch horror movies, so the thought felt like it came out of nowhere. But then again, running through the mountains in the dark, slogging through a 100-mile course with 21,000 feet of elevation gain in order to get a "free" belt buckle is borderline psychopathic behavior according to most sane people. So maybe thinking about fictional movie psychopaths isn't that out of line.

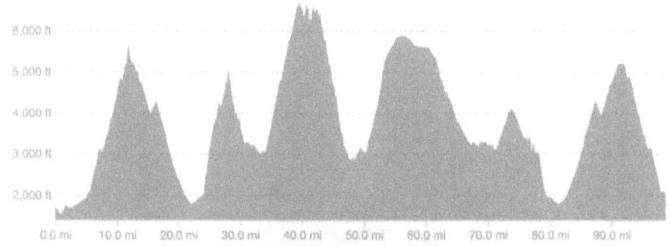

The Hellbender 100, set in the Black Mountains of North Carolina, billed itself as the "hardest and highest 100 on the East Coast," with five climbs of 3,000 feet or more. In order to sign up, you're required to have completed at least one other 100-mile race, and the 2019 race was only the second year of the event, so it would be hard to end up running in the Hellbender by accident. But I kind of did.

My friend Forest had signed up, and I was supposed to pace him for the last 30 miles, so I'd planned a whole trip around it: pace Forest in the Hellbender, meet my dad in Atlanta a couple days later to catch a Braves game, then head to Alabama to tour the music studios at Muscle Shoals.

Then Forest injured his foot and it wasn't healed a month before the race. I half-joked to him that I could just run in his place:

> **To:** Forest Woodward
>
> *Mar 10, 2019, 3:54 PM*
>
> Man glad to hear it on the knee front! Foot is still flaring for me on runs. Pretty disappointing. Don't think I'm going to make hellbender. Have you booked tickets yet? Let me know how much I owe you. Sorry to be a lame duck. Hoping we can do something big together on foot together this summer at least.
>
> Ah bummer! Yeah I booked tickets a while back, no worries. We can crew for Canyon or volunteer at aid stations or something. Or I can get a wig and pretend I'm you and just go for it

Of course, a half joke is also half not a joke, and a couple emails later, I was signed up for the race myself, with 80 other people. Including Forest's brother, Canyon, who is much faster. To say I was running the Hellbender 100 with Canyon is similar to saying that, if you happened to be somewhere on El Capitan when Alex Honnold free soloed Freerider, that you climbed El Cap with Alex Honnold.

At the starting line of the race at Camp Grier, at 4:30 a.m. on April 12, Canyon and I posed for a quick photo together, and I said, "Canyon, I was thinking. Do you want to run the first 15 …

…

… feet together?" He laughed, and when we were called to make our way to the starting arch, went to the front of the pack. I went to the back of the pack, futzing with my headlamp to turn it from the red light setting to white light, and failing. Hilary, my wife, finally handed me her headlamp and I jogged off, in 81st place out of 81 runners. I'm not sure if it's the right strategy or not, but I figured if I was going to make it through all 100 miles, it'd be best not to take off too fast, or, really, fast at all. We jogged along a dark asphalt road for the first five miles, and I passed a few people, but mostly just shuffled along, hoping it wouldn't rain all day.

A couple miles later, the rain started, as runners started to spread out on our climb up to The Pinnacle, 4,000 vertical feet up in the first 12 miles of the race. It drizzled, then poured rain, so we were totally soaked, as well as socked in by clouds, so no views. I settled into a rhythm of hiking uphill at a conversational pace, then jogging downhills and flats where I could—and finding that the course was quite technical.

The rain let up, and so did the climbing, sending us down a wide dirt road for a six-mile descent into the aid station at 23.5 miles. As I started climbing up the next section, a 3,300-foot climb to the Blue Ridge Parkway, I thought of my joke about "we have to switch to ultrarunning now" whenever I crossed the 26.2 mark, from marathon distance to ultramarathon distance. I could see one guy about 100 feet ahead of me, but other than him, no one was around to laugh at the joke, which was OK, because it's not that funny, and certainly much less funny when you're hiking straight uphill and still have 73-point-something miles to go.

--

I had never considered myself much of a runner, especially not a distance runner. On my high school track team, the distance guys were built like deer—lean, long, and able to grit out the pain of running the mile at a blistering pace. I had a different relationship with suffering at that point, telling my coach that anything over 200 meters was long-distance, at least to me. He put me in the 400-meter run a couple times and I think realized there were probably much better candidates for the job when I kept up with the other runners respectably until about 250 meters, when my lane appeared to fill with invisible quicksand and the pack ran away from me as I struggled to keep my legs moving until the finish line. I rode out the rest of my track career running 4 x 100 and 4 x 200 relays, and then went to college, eventually giving up running for partying, and then a pack-a-day smoking habit for six years.

I tried to quit smoking more than 25,000 times, as smokers do, and eventually decided to enter a marathon in 2006 to motivate myself. It worked: I trained for the race for six months, I quit smoking, and after the marathon, quit running marathons too, giving myself a nice nine-year break from distance running. Aside from the occasional trail run, I climbed, hiked, and backpacked and managed to stay in shape. Nine years later, I signed up for my first 50K, coming to ultrarunning not as a runner, but as a climber, hiker, and mountaineer.

I was 36 when I did that first ultramarathon, 38 when I finished my first 100-mile race, and by that time, had spent more time in the mountains than I ever could have dreamed. I hadn't learned so much about trail running, but a lot about how to keep moving when everything hurt, how to take care of myself, and how to get home safely. I looked at ultramarathons not so much as opportunities to race against other people, but as a way to test my limits with some support—with a marked course, some food and water stops along the way, and a pacer for the final miles, you could shut off parts of your brain and just go, focusing on moving forward and seeing what you learn from grinding it out when things get really bleak.

--

It was right around mile 40, walking through the woods on the Black Mountain Crest Trail between the summits of Mt. Mitchell and Mt. Craig, that I felt all of the time I'd spent climbing, hiking, running, and faffing around in the mountains paid off. I had my trekking poles tucked under one arm, was eating a thawed but not warm burrito with both hands, and I had to use the bathroom. Except the bathroom was at the last aid station, a mile backwards and uphill and in my past, which is not an ideal location for a bathroom when you're running a 100-mile ultramarathon you're not sure you can finish. Also not ideal: being halfway through eating a burrito you really want to finish when you have to go No. 2. But I was prepared for this situation.

I ducked off the trail, walked 100 feet into the woods, stuffed my burrito in my vest pocket for afterward, pulled out a half-buried rock, dug underneath it with a stick, and did my thing. Two minutes later, I was back on the trail, eating my burrito, and here is how that's not gross: I always keep a single latex glove and an individually-wrapped wet wipe in the glove. When situations like this pop up and I'm trail running, I pull the latex glove on, take care of things, and hold the used wipe with the gloved fingers as I pull the glove off by turning it inside out. Then I knot the inside-out glove, trash sealed safely inside, and tuck it back in my vest to throw in the trash later. In events in which handwashing opportunities are nonexistent and you have to eat once or twice an hour, I highly recommend this method to help keep you from getting sick.

I jogged into the Colbert Creek aid station at Mile 48 just as the last light of the day was disappearing around 8:20 p.m., feeling good after jogging some big sections of the trail for the previous five miles, as opposed to walking. Although it had been slow going (the slowest 50-mile split I've ever recorded), I reminded myself that these things always take way longer than I assume they're going to, while I changed my socks and packed a wind jacket, rain jacket, and liner gloves into my vest for the next 24 miles into the night.

A guy I ran with a little bit on the last section had said

the second half of the course was easier, and the lady parked next to Hilary said it was "more runnable," but I was not counting my chickens before they hatched. Even if it was all flat terrain for the second half of the race, I was pretty sure I would find a way to feel like shit at some point. Hilary walked me partway down the road to the next section of trail, another 3,000-foot climb up the Buncombe Horse Trail.

In the thick trees, under the clouds, without many stars visible, I settled into an almost complete darkness, pacing myself uphill, not knowing where the top of the climb would actually be. I didn't see another headlamp for over an hour on the way up, then finally started catching a few folks on a set of switchbacks. One guy asked as I passed, "that next aid station's gotta be coming up pretty soon, doesn't it?" I told him I couldn't say, and I tried to keep myself from thinking the same thing he'd asked. I could drive myself crazy straining to locate for signs of an aid station up the trail: the tiny dots of headlamps, the faint din of music, maybe the glow of a fire if they had one going? It was best not to think about it, because if I started wishing it was there, I'd start wishing every minute, then feeling sorry for myself.

I caught up to Ryan, a guy from Raleigh, and we jogged and hiked as the steep climb flattened out. Any relief at the end of the steep climbing was dashed when we discovered that the trail had, thanks to rain, become a trough of mud and standing water. At first we tried to hop around the wet sections, and then, realizing it was unavoidable, just walked through it, as it soaked our shoes. Here's the point where if I could give myself advice, I'd say, "Hey, while you're putting that rain jacket in your vest, pack an extra pair of socks to change into," because immediately, the moisture started causing blisters on the bottoms of both feet.

We separated after the aid station, and I ran and hiked alone for a long time, still feeling like I had a lot left in the tank even though I was moving more slowly than I had hoped. Around 2:30 in the morning, I had my psycho-killer-coming-out-of-the-woods daydream, but besides that, I just kept trucking down the mountain, stopping at the aid station at Mile 65 to eat some avocado rolls and potatoes. Six miles, I reminded myself, and I'd be done running by myself—Hilary was in the rental car at the next aid station and would pace me for the last 28 miles. The six miles, as I fantasized, was not all downhill, and trudging through a short climb, I started to feel my morale dip. I told myself I'd ask Hilary to let me sleep for 15 minutes at the next aid station, and that would help. Then I realized I hadn't ingested any caffeine in several hours, and popped a few caffeinated Clif Bloks into my mouth, almost instantly feeling a little bit better, or at least not on the verge of curling up in the fetal position on the side of the trail to have a good cry and a nap.

--

Leaving the Neals Creek aid station at Mile 71.5, after 24 hours, I joked to the volunteer checking me out: "How far am I off the lead runners?" Obviously a guy who was very used to sarcasm, he acknowledged the joke with a nod and no laughter, replying, "Well, they finished two and half hours ago, so …" Canyon had finished a half-hour earlier, despite having bonked at Mile 70 and struggling to finish, still taking third place. He would, by my calculations, be able to have a leisurely meal, a nice long night of sleep, and another leisurely meal before I crossed the finish line.

Hilary and I hiked up the road and onto singletrack as I shoved huge bites of pizza into my mouth, hoping the 1,000-foot climb up to the Blue Ridge Parkway would fly by. We had talked about the strategy for this part of the race, and it had been pretty simple: 1) make me jog as much as possible, even if we're "running" 17-minute miles; 2) make me eat; and 3) don't let me sit down. The sun started to rise as we climbed.

After we crested the Blue Ridge Parkway, my feet really started to hurt, in a way that was brand-new to my experience: I had blisters on the balls of my feet where they met my toes, and on some of the bottoms of my toes, and the movement of walking and running started to shoot pain from my feet up into my legs.

I had done little research on the individual sections of trail, only focusing on the big climbs: 4,000 feet here, 3,000 feet there, 1,000 feet, 3,500 feet, et cetera. When we started up the Leadmine Gap Trail about Mile 77, we were greeted by a series of three climbs you could interpret as "Haha, surprise!" or "Fuck you": only 100 or 150 feet each, they were 25 percent grade, which my feet and legs felt like, to be honest, was asking a bit much at this point. Hilary led and I tried to follow as closely as possible now gritting my teeth as the pain in my feet became almost constant. Surrounding us: panoramic views of the Blue Ridge Mountains, which I promised myself would be there to enjoy more fully some other time, or just to enjoy at all some other time.

At the Curtis Creek aid station at mile 80.1, they had pancakes, and let me tell you, if you ever forget how fucking great pancakes are, I cannot recommend highly enough running and hiking 80 miles as fast as you can, and then having some very nice person who has stayed up all night or gotten up early of their own volition serve you a couple very basic pancakes with syrup on a disposable plate. Even if you are the type of person who likes to go out to a restaurant just waiting and hoping for something, anything, to be slightly wrong so you can write up a shitty Yelp review when you get home, I believe pancakes at Mile 80 will turn you from the Grinch into a true believer. They may bring you back from the dead for a few minutes.

However, you still have 20 more miles to cover, so the joy is fleeting. Hilary and I jogged down two miles of road before the next climb, 2600 feet up to the Blue Ridge Parkway. Midway up the climb, I was starting to let out audible grunts as I exhaled, as it seemed to make the pain in my feet a little less intense. As the dirt road ended and singletrack began, we started chatting with another runner. He was a bit dismayed that the last aid station was out of cheese for quesadillas, and that someone had said to him that this was the easiest part of the race, and how could it be the easiest part of the race if there was this big climb that we were now headed up and then following that, a very long and technical downhill section ...

At this point, I noticed Hilary had shifted gears and was beginning to pull away. I dug deep and tried to catch her, and within a few minutes, we were out of earshot. Hilary said, "Sorry, I just think we should get away from—"

"Yup," I said. I already had enough negative voices in my head; I didn't need one more. We stepped over a guardrail, crossed the Blue Ridge Parkway, and jogged a brief downhill to begin the last half-marathon of the race.

--

In February 2020, the *New York Times Magazine* published a story about ultrarunner Jim Walmsley, who had qualified for the U.S. Olympic Trials, and whether he could transfer his dominance of longer distances on trails to a road marathon. In the piece, Joseph Bien-Kahn writes:

"Because athleticism is only part of the equation in races that are just as much about your tolerance for extreme mental and physical strain, mainstream runners often look down on the ultra-runner. They still see a field of eccentrics and seekers, pushing their bodies and minds, which is well and good but certainly not a sport. (Some people in the distance-running community derisively refer to ultra-runners as 'hobby joggers' or 'glorified fast-walkers.')"

I had never heard those terms before, but laughed when I read them, as well as a couple other terms Bieh-Kahn used to refer to ultrarunners in the piece—"masochistic oddballs" and "amateur challenge-seekers," which I can't argue are untrue descriptions. When I first started running ultramarathons, I looked around at the starting line, and sure, there were a few ultra-fit looking folks, but the rest of us sure don't look like we're going to hoof out a sub-3-hour marathon. But I guess if we wanted to run a marathon, we would do that. And lots of us do: the same year I ran the Hellbender 100, I ran three other ultramarathons and three road marathons, including the New York City Marathon.

I had fun at all of the races, ultramarathons and marathons alike. All of them sucked at times. In one race, I was running with 53,000 other people, with thousands of people cheering, and music playing every few miles. In another race, I was in a dense, dark forest in the mountains of North Carolina, trusting myself not to trip on tree roots and rocks, and not seeing another person for an hour or more. I love trail ultramarathons, and road marathons, but I have to say, when you all of a sudden find yourself in urgent need of a restroom, it's pretty nice not to have to wait in line at a port-a-potty while the clock is ticking, and just hop off into the trees somewhere.

I came into ultrarunning not from road running, but climbing and mountaineering, which can also be endurance sports, but come with a completely different set of hazards. After several years of climbing, I wanted to take a break from the feeling of danger and just push myself in the outdoors, so ultrarunning was an easy transition. I often joke that ultrarunning is all the pain and suffering of mountaineering without the fear of death, which I think is mostly true. In mountaineering, you spend a lot of time thinking about the ways you could die and utilizing techniques and equipment to minimize the odds of death. In ultrarunning, not very many people die, but lots of people feel like they're going to die, for a not-insignificant portion of the time they're ultrarunning.

I've realized that I like being out on a trail for 20 miles during a training run, or 30 miles, or even 50 miles. I mostly don't pay attention to how long it takes me, unless I've promised to be home at a certain time. I just go out and move for several hours, never looking at my phone, and when I finish running, I have burned enough calories to justify eating half a deep-dish pizza. Masochistic? Sure. Oddball? That's fair, too. When you show up at an ultramarathon, though, you feel less like an oddball, with all the other masochistic oddballs around.

--

Hilary kept me moving, up the final climb across the Blue Ridge Parkway, and down the technical descent to the finish line. I kept searching the trees below for a sign of the finish arch, a little bit of red somewhere, and of course it seemed like it was never going to appear. The last seven miles was almost completely downhill, dropping 3,000 feet, and it took us two hours. I had told myself there was no need to run the final few hundred feet through the finish arch—I mean, after 36 hours, what was the point of rushing to shave off a few seconds? But then, we stepped off the trail onto the grass, and I said to Hilary, OK, we can jog. So we did.

10

A CASE FOR THE APPLE FRITTER AS ENDURANCE FUEL

Occasionally—not all the time—as someone who fancies himself a writer, I make decisions based on the idea that something I do might end up in a story somewhere. This piece is an example of that. Plus I was honestly hungry, and am pretty used to eating while running, plus the donut shop was literally right on the race course, so it wasn't that outlandish. Basically, I would have done it anyway, story or not. But, of course, I did end up writing about it.

--

At about Mile 13 of the Colfax Marathon, I was starting to feel hungry. I did the math in my head—I had about 14 miles of running left, and one remaining package of Clif Bloks in my handheld water bottle. I could very probably make it to the finish line on those Clif Bloks, plus maybe a couple pieces of bananas and/or a Honey Stinger gel handed out by volunteers. And that would be fine.

Or, I could run into Winchell's, which was literally less than 100 feet off the race course just after Mile 17, and get an apple fritter. And that would be much tastier.

Look: I have nothing against "space food," the stuff we commonly eat while doing endurance events. I have consumed hundreds of gels, blocks, waffles, and thousands of ounces of electrolyte drinks. They do the job, and lots of them taste pretty good, or decent enough that you don't hate them until you've eaten about 50 of them over the course of a few months or a year and you just get sick of them. A non-scientific chart of enjoyment of space food products might look like this:

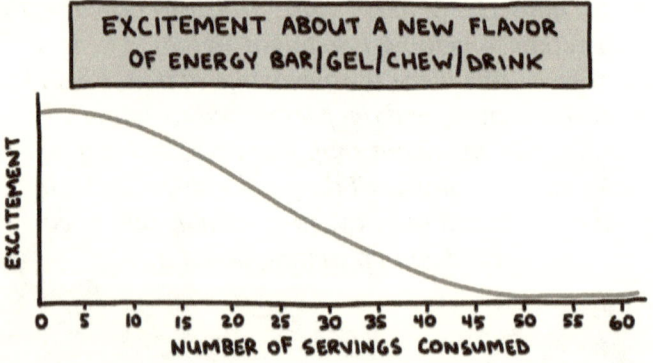

This is no fault of energy bar companies—they do great work, and I applaud them for that. But when your product is designed to be sold to people doing really uncomfortable things, you can't expect those people to make lifelong commitments to your Lemon-Lime flavor of energy semi-solids. Pizza, or ballpark hot dogs, are a much easier sell: Both are most often associated with positive memories. You eat pizza while having good times with your friends, a ballpark hot dog while at a game with your family—not while exerting yourself for four to 36 hours on a bicycle or running trail, cramming calories into your mouth more to avoid bonking than for any sort of epicurean enjoyment.

Energy foods, on the other hand, are harder to associate with positive memories. You don't cross a finish line, high-five your friends and family, gather yourself, and then sit down at a restaurant to look over the menu and then decide maybe you'll just have a few more of those tasty energy globules and gels instead of a plate of nachos or a cheeseburger. Hell no you don't. You smash that cheeseburger. And the nachos.

But those energy foods have served their purpose, which, as far as my personal research goes, is two-pronged: a) they provide readily available caloric fuel so you can continue moving, and b) they don't make you shit your pants while exercising. If you do enough endurance activities, you probably have used your own trial-and-error process to figure out what meets both a) and b), and have a few things you rely on fairly regularly.

OK then. But have you ever eaten an apple fritter in the middle of an endurance activity? If you haven't, I recommend it, as part of your trial-and-error process (if it causes the aforementioned digestive issues, obviously the rest of this piece is not going to be relevant for you). I'm not saying you should eat one every time you go out for a run longer than 10 miles or a bike ride longer than 30 miles, but every once in a while, it's pretty damn good for morale. And, of course, good for calories, which most of us require to sustain life.

Nowadays, if you have an idea about nutrition, you can

probably find an article or study out there to support it, or at least someone with a pretty large social media following. For longer-distance events, lots of smart people agree that a human body requires carbohydrates—which you can find in apple fritters and energy blocks alike:

NUTRITIONAL COMPARISON	APPLE FRITTER	BRAND X ENERGY CHEWS (1 PACKAGE)
CALORIES	600	200
CARBS	93 GRAMS	48 GRAMS
SUGAR	39 GRAMS	24 GRAMS
PROTEIN	8 GRAMS	0 GRAMS
FAT	23 GRAMS	0 GRAMS
SODIUM	690 MG	100 MG

Some experts think a small amount of protein is good during endurance events, some don't. Most experts agree that electrolytes need to be replaced during endurance events, especially if you're sweating heavily—and our friend the apple fritter contains 690 milligrams of sodium, or a little more than twice the amount in a single serving of Tailwind.

Note that an entire apple fritter contains 600 calories, which is probably way too many to eat all at once while running or cycling, no matter who you ask. I suggest: Eating half of the apple fritter, or 300 calories. Splitting it with a friend is ideal, as the portability of an apple fritter is a bit limited, at least when compared to energy chews. But it is possible to carry an apple fritter in a bag for quite a while, or at least until you're hungry again. This all depends on motivation and your personal dedication to that fritter.

OTHER CONSIDERATIONS	APPLE FRITTER	BRAND X ENERGY CHEWS
CALORIE-DENSE	YES	YES
EASY TO CHEW	YES	YES
EASY TO CARRY	NOT REALLY	YES
TASTY	YES	KIND OF
CONTAINS CAFFEINE	NO	SOMETIMES
GETS SMOOSHED	YES	NOT REALLY

As we approached Mile 17 of the Colfax Marathon, I pulled my credit card from my pocket and held it in my hand, so at least it wouldn't be covered in sweat when I handed it to the cashier at Winchell's. A few hundred feet from the building, I picked up my pace a bit, hoping to gain a few seconds and compensate for the net loss of time I'd experience in the donut shop. I popped through the door, delighted to see no line, and ordered an apple fritter. Less than 60 seconds later, I was back outside, jogging with my bagged pastry. For a time comparison, when I stopped at a port-a-potty at Mile 4, my total time including a wait behind four people was about two minutes and 30 seconds.

I re-joined my wife and we continued our previous pace. I slid the fritter out of the bag and took bites as we ran, downing half of it in about a half-mile of running. It was fresh, soft, sweet, and didn't have an overly-fried taste that some apple fritters have.

We finished the race feeling relatively strong, and I clocked my second-best marathon time ever, using a combination of energy blocks and a donut. Now, was this a well-designed, controlled experiment? No. Does this offer any proof besides anecdotal evidence that apple fritters can work as endurance fuel? Also no.

Could you, however, through your own trial-and-error process, decide if apple fritters are right for you? Yes. If you don't really like apple fritters, could you use another donut in its place? Hey, this is a free country—you can attempt an Ironman triathlon with a turkey leg in your hand if you want to. All I'm saying is there are other options beyond traditional endurance foods, including donuts.

11

THE HILL THAT YOU LOVE TO HATE

Maybe you've had a moment like this: You're driving a car you've had for a long time, maybe on your way to work one day, and you start mentally cataloguing all the things that are wrong with it: That hole in the seat, that funny noise it makes when you turn left, that stain on the ceiling, the window you can't roll down because it won't go back up again, the crack in the windshield, the small dent in the passenger door, et cetera. You think, "Wow, this car's kind of a piece of shit." And you think about it for another second or two, and then you have the thought, "But it's my piece of shit." And maybe you rub the dashboard a little bit with one of your hands, as if it were a loyal pet. That's kind of how I feel about the hill in this story.

--

"I hate this hill," I said to the man pushing his mountain bike up the dirt road. He was trying to tell me that it was his age, 75, holding him back from pedaling the whole 750-foot climb in a mile, but I felt I should assure him that it sucks regardless of your age. "I think it's actually worse biking it than running it."

Officially, this stretch of road is part of the Green

Mountain Trail, officially in the William Frederick Hayden Park on Green Mountain, which I'm pretty sure everyone calls "Green Mountain." If you were visiting Denver, and had half a day to hike, would I take you on a two-mile hike up this road? Hell no. Within earshot, you have two freeways (I-70 and C-470), a shooting range, a motocross track, and a drag racing track. There's no shade. It's steep—at one point, it hits a 22% grade, according to TrailRunProject.

I don't know if I truly hate it, but I definitely love/hate it. I like to think most of us have a hill like this in our lives, that they go to for a workout that's better than hiking up a concrete stairwell inside a high-rise building, but just barely.

I have encountered dozens of people on this same one-mile stretch of trail that isn't even really a trail—it's an access road to the top of Green Mountain, wide enough to drive a pickup on (which official people do), or, occasionally, an ambulance (which I've seen once). Tons of Denver metro area residents use it—hikers, walkers, trail runners, mountain bikers—and if you asked any of us to say something nice about it, it would probably be, "There's a nice view of the city at the top." On good days, you can see three Fourteeners from the top too—Longs Peak, Mt. Evans, and Pikes Peak. And maybe some elk and deer. But that's a best-case scenario. Usually it's just hot, steep, and not very wilderness-y.

And yet, this year alone, I've already hiked and run this stretch of road more than 60 times. Why? Well, it's the easiest place to get in a bunch of vertical climbing on a non-pavement surface, if you need that sort of thing, which I happen to. It's one of the first things that's dry after a snowstorm or a rainstorm, and even if it's not dry, there's only so much damage you can do to a wide dirt road by hiking and running on it, considering it's built to handle the weight of a truck. So most of us play it safe by using the road instead of nearby singletrack when the trailhead sign says conditions are muddy.

When I'm out there, under the baking afternoon sun, or alternately slogging through occasional mud and occasionally postholing through a bit of snow in mid-winter, I always see someone else doing the same thing, in a pair of hiking boots, trail running shoes, or on a mountain bike. One guy hikes it with hand crutches, one lady runs up it faster than I can run down it (and then repeats it several times), and lots of people bring dogs. We all hear the faint whoosh of freeway traffic, sometimes the braaap of motorcycles in the motocross park across the street, and sometimes the rat-a-tat-tat of someone popping off shots at the shooting range next to the motocross park. And sometimes thunder from a storm rolling over the high mountains a few miles to the west.

I go up, I go down, and then I repeat. One time, training for a long race in the mountains, I did 14 laps, and just as I was really hating the shit out of it somewhere around Lap 12, a guy who had seen me doing the same thing for a couple hours asked, "What are you training for?" I blurted out, "Something way worse," which was only partially true. I was training for something way longer, but not nearly as boring.

Is it mind-numbing? I don't know. I seem to have enough to think about while I'm going uphill and looking forward to the downhill, and then going downhill and dreading the next uphill, and periodically counting how many laps I have left. It's repetitive, yes. Boring, sure. Sometimes I do it for a couple hours, sometimes four or five hours, and occasionally, eight or 10 hours. I hate that hill. But I keep going back, up and down that hill, so it can't be that bad, right?

I mean, one time last winter, I ran for an hour on a treadmill, indoors, the only scenery two TVs in front of me, one showing an alarmist news commentary show and the other showing a cooking show designed around (I believe) a diet plan to fast-track you to coronary artery disease. THAT sucked. Give me my muddy, snowy, road up the hill by the freeway any day.

12

THE BIGHORN 100: A RACE REPORT

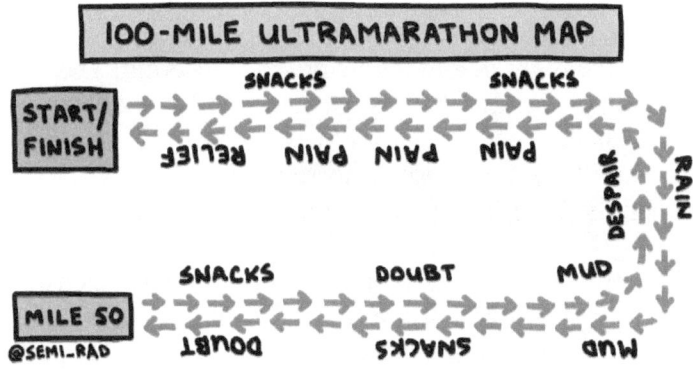

The Bighorn 100 was my third 100-mile ultramarathon. In the year following my first 100-mile race, the Run Rabbit Run 100, I had started thinking about doing another 100-miler, just to prove to myself that I could do it again. The Bighorn seemed to check a lot of boxes: Relatively close to where we lived (6.5-hour drive from Denver), lots of elevation gain (18,000+ feet), a new-to-me mountain range, a different state (Wyoming), and more than a few people recommended it as a good race. It was supposed to be my second 100-miler, until I tricked myself into running the Hellbender 100 (Chapter 9), and after that experience, I thought,

> *"At least the Bighorn won't be THAT bad." And you know what? It was just differently bad.*

--

Here's something you don't really want to hear the week before you run a 100-mile race you're not sure you can finish: The course has so much mud and snow on it this year that the race directors will give everyone an extra hour to complete the race.

Also, the night before, at the pre-race meeting: The section of the trail they usually say has "shoe-sucking mud" is now being referred to as "horse-sucking mud" because they almost lost a horse there a few days prior when the horse plunged into the mud up to its belly.

The Bighorn 100 is known for a lot of things: beautiful scenery, wonderful organizers and volunteers, lots of elevation gain (somewhere between 18,000 and 20,000 feet of climbing), and sometimes, slick mud. I signed up for the race back in January because a) it was in June and I wouldn't have to take up my whole summer training for it, b) it's in northern Wyoming, only about six hours from where I live, and c) I had a fuzzy memory of my friend Matt Trappe telling me it was fun when he ran it four or five years ago. At least I think he said "fun."

The night before the race, at our Airbnb in Sheridan, Wyoming, about 30 minutes from the race start near the town of Dayton, I was more worried about overdoing it in the heat than about the mud. "Mud, I can handle," I foolishly told myself, popping a melatonin and lying down for what I hoped would be 6.5 hours of sleep.

The next morning, we drove to Scott Park in Dayton and boarded school buses taking us up the Tongue River Canyon to the starting line, and stood on the gravel canyon road for a few minutes awaiting the 9 a.m. start. I stood near the back of the pack and reviewed my goals, in order of priority:

- Don't die
- Say thank you to all aid station volunteers you encounter
- Don't complain
- Finish the race before the 35-hour cutoff
- If possible, finish faster than 35 hours
- Don't sit down at more than five aid stations total
- Don't sit down for more than five minutes unless you're changing socks
- Run all the downhills until at least Mile 70; hike the rest as fast as you can
- Don't get hungry
- Avoid serious injury

We jogged and walked up 1.25 miles of road to the Tongue River Canyon trailhead, where we switched to singletrack, and I ran into a couple local guys I know, Chris and Steve. I hiked and chatted with them for the entire first climb up the canyon, 3,300 vertical feet in seven miles. I had told myself that if I soaked the front of my shirt in sweat in the first climb, I would be screwed, as it would be impossible to replace all the fluids I lost. And of course, hiking fast to keep up with Chris and Steve, I was very near soaking my shirt in sweat. Thankfully, we dropped downhill at about 7,500 feet and I cooled off a little bit, and went off on my own pace.

The people who said the course was beautiful were right—the route is essentially a tour of canyons with high limestone cliffs dotting the sides, and alpine meadows. Lots of it is open and exposed to the sun until about Mile 30, but breezes and a couple rain showers and thunderstorms kept me cool.

At about mile 9, I started jogging down a faded two-track road and all of a sudden felt the left side of my running vest become really loose, bouncing every time I took a step. I knew what had happened: Several weeks prior, I'd noticed the cord holding the left side of the vest together fraying. The core of the cord had remained intact, and I, an idiot, had figured it would be fine. I also didn't bring another vest, even though my crew (my wife, Hilary, and friend Jayson) would be meeting me at Mile 30 and 66. I kept walking, pulled my vest off and tried to juggle it and my trekking poles as I figured out how to jury-rig the whole thing to last another 91 miles. After trying to tie it together twice, I looked down and realized my race bib was pinned to my shorts with four safety pins, which have heroically been holding things together since 1849, and, it struck me, might be able to do the job here in the Bighorn 100 as well. I pinned my vest together, ran about a quarter-mile, and forgot about it.

I rolled through the next few aid stations, stopping only to fill my bottles with water and Tailwind, always checking my watch to make sure I got in and out in less than two minutes. At about Mile 14, the course jogged up and down small inclines for about 10 miles, and I hiked the uphills and ran the downhills, chatting a bit with a few runners, including Sergio from South Carolina, who was running his first 100-mile race, and Larry from Pennsylvania, who had been running competitively since the 1970s and has done dozens of ultras. For a solid hour, we were harassed by rain and increasingly loud thunder, which got as close as about two miles away, and then moved away.

At 25 miles, the trail started to drop, gradually and then steeply, losing about 2,500 vertical feet before Mile 30. Up until this point I had seen little mud, but knew the forecast called for more rain, and wondered what the steep downhill section would be like on the way back the next morning.

I jogged into the 30-mile aid station just under the eight-hour mark to meet up with Hilary and Jayson, wipe off my feet and change my socks. My list of "Things I Need You To Make Me Do That I Might Not Want To Do (Or Remember To Do) at the 30-Mile Aid Station" read:

- Eat a banana
- Drink a protein drink
- Refill food in vest (5 waffles, 6 bloks, 2 pie bars)
- Pack two slices of pizza in vest
- Put extra headlamp in vest
- Put pants in vest
- Put wind jacket in vest

At 30 miles, I felt OK. A headache from dehydration

(took off too fast on the first sunny climb), but no major aches and pains, no hot spots, and no chafing. As I took off from the aid station, it started to downpour, soaking me through as I started a steady, 4,200-foot climb over the next 15 miles. Soon enough, I passed the Cathedral Rock aid station at Mile 33.5, then the Spring Marsh aid station at Mile 40, as the sun set and the light slowly dimmed around me.

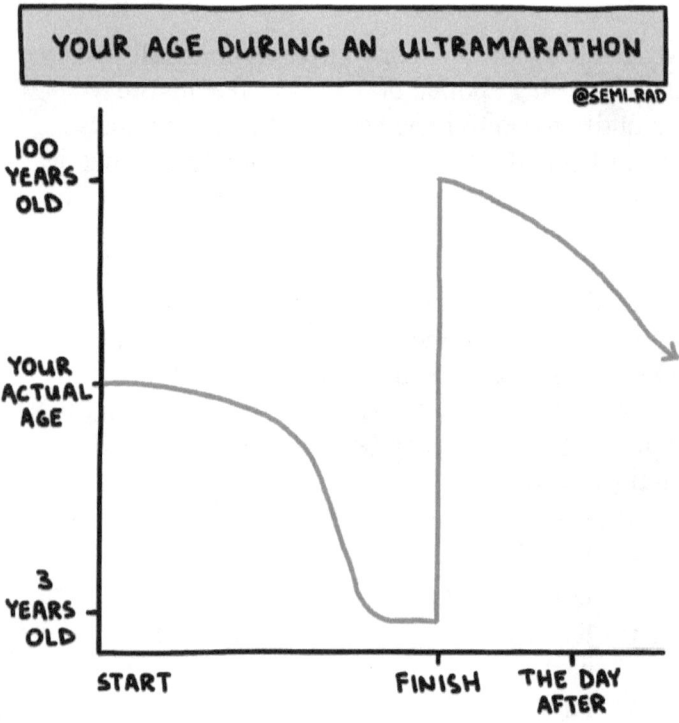

A mile or two after the Spring Marsh aid station, the trail entered an aspen stand, the entire floor of which seemed to be mud. I picked my way around, trying to keep my shoes clean and dry, succeeding for the most part. Almost out the other side, a runner came back through the forest toward me—he was near the front of the pack, headed down already. He saw me tiptoeing through the muck and said, "Don't worry, there's plenty more of that ahead." Foolishly, I thought, "How bad could it be?"

At the Elk Camp aid station (Mile 43.5), I filled my water bottles and continued up, clicking on my headlamp. I suppose you could say this is where the bullshit started. When you think of mud, you probably think about it being messy, wet, maybe even sticky. The mud of the Bighorn Mountains is not sticky. I had actually read about it on the internet before the race, while doing a little research on what to expect. People said it was slick. People were right about that.

Most of the way up, it wasn't that horrible. I had read previous reports of people saying they took two steps up and would slide one step back—at the time I was headed uphill, it wasn't that bad. I slid around a bit, lost my footing a lot, and in general used way more energy than I would have if the trail was dry, or even less wet. My shoes and socks got completely soaked, and it was getting colder as I gained elevation, but I figured I'd be OK if I just kept moving.

The route between miles 43.5 and about mile 45.5 was mostly just a quagmire, a 10- or 20-foot wide path of marshy, muddy footprints. I gave up and started plowing through the mud, having given up on dry feet or clean shoes. Then some snow started to appear, and for the most part, I could trod across a dirty path where others had already tamped it down. But then I stepped shin-deep, both feet, into icy water that couldn't have been warmer than 32.1 degrees Fahrenheit. I paused, shocked at how cold my feet were now, and wondered if the rest of my body would follow suit. For about 60 seconds, I was pretty sure I was fucked. I had no dry shoes or socks until Mile 66, which, at my pace, was six hours away. Unable to do anything else, I shrugged and kept plodding uphill.

Eventually, I came to a man holding a flashlight in the middle of nowhere, and he told me to continue across a dirt road, where I'd see the rest of the marked trail. Then another man with a flashlight, and a few minutes later I arrived at the heated tents at the Jaws aid station, Mile 48, at 8,800 feet above sea level, 11:15 p.m. If I wanted to, I could sit next to a heater, dry my clothes, eat a ton of food, get really comfortable, and take a nice nap. Also, I could quit the race—because after I did all that nice stuff and got comfortable, if I didn't quit, I'd have to go right back down all that mud and snow I just wallowed through.

I sat down for four minutes, a saint of a man brought me a cheese quesadilla, I fished around in my vest and found my beanie, filled my water bottles, and got up and left. It was cold, and I was in shorts, a wind jacket, and a rain jacket, with both jacket hoods up and cinched, and it was just enough clothing to keep me warm if I kept moving. My headache from earlier in the day had disappeared, thanks to drinking lots of fluids, so on the spectrum of Feeling Like Shit to Feeling Fine, I was just over the halfway mark, slightly closer to Feeling Fine.

I started to gradually descend, and the course markers led me back into the woods, the mud, and the snow. I postholed in some of the same places, sort of flash-freezing my feet in the icy water again, and clenched my teeth for a second while I kept moving. I slid all over the place, worse than going uphill, at times feeling like I was wearing penny loafers while trying to walk down a ski slope. It sucked, but it was just going to suck as long as I was in it, so I kept going.

I kept thinking of the Russian spy character played by Mark Rylance in *Bridge of Spies*, when Tom Hanks keeps asking him if he's worried the Russians will kill him. He replies very calmly more than once, "Would it help?" as in, "would it actually change anything if I worried?" Complain, get mad, get sad, cry, whatever—none of it was going to dry the mud, or my feet.

I passed a lot of runners on their way uphill as I made my way downhill, wondering if they were thinking the same thing I was on my way up: that I would have to go right back down through this mess in a few minutes. I was solidly in the middle of the pack, so I'd been passed by 100-plus faster runners going the other way on my way up, and I passed 100-plus runners going the other way on my way down, as well as a handful of their pacers.

Probably around Mile 51 inbound/Mile 45 outbound, as I was negotiating another slick/steep section, I slipped, barely catching myself without falling, probably looking very much like a cartoon character. At the exact same time, an uphill runner about 15 feet from me slipped and fell into the mud, catching herself on one arm and narrowly avoiding a total mud bath. As she got up, she yelled, "Jesus Goddamn Christ, Shit, FUCK!" Which is basically the same feeling I was having, and probably almost everyone else in the race was too. I told her there was more mud ahead, but a nice warm tent at the top of the climb. Not that that helped our current situation, I guess.

I eventually made it through what I thought would be the worst of the mud, popping into the next couple aid stations to refill my bottles and then jogging and hiking the rest of the descent to the Mile 66 aid station, where I would meet my crew. I had lofty hopes of arriving there while it was still dark, but the sun came up in the last hour of my descent, gradually lighting the canyon around me as I shuffled along next to the Little Bighorn River. A lot of people say the night is the most depressing time of a 100-mile race, but I actually hate the sunrise the most—probably because I'm slow and it's a sign that I've already been going almost 24 hours but still have several more hours to go.

I jogged into the Sally's Footbridge aid station, Mile 66, at almost exactly 5:30 a.m., and sat down for about 15 minutes to change socks and shoes—my shoes, socks, and lower legs were now coated in mud a few millimeters thick. My list of "Things I Need You To Make Me Do That I Might Not Want To Do (Or Remember To Do) at the 66-Mile Aid Station":

- Eat a banana
- Drink a protein drink
- Refill food in vest (5 waffles, 6 bloks, 2 pie bars)
- Pack two slices of pizza in vest
- Apply sunscreen
- Take phone charger + cable

- Ditch pants and wind jacket
- Ditch headlamp

I would not be the first person to say that people who pace and crew ultrarunners are heroes. By the time I jogged into this aid station, Hilary and Jayson had been awake for two and half hours, getting up at 3 a.m. just in case I was having the race of my life and managed to get from mile 30 to 66 in 10.5 hours. That didn't quite happen.

But Hilary was waiting, standing at the check-in tent looking up the trail for me when I got there, and Jayson was ready to start running because he knows showing up is 75 percent of friendship. We started the steep uphill climb out of Sally's Footbridge just before 6 a.m.—hour 21 for me. I trudged up the trail, dry at first. Then there appeared sections of mud that weren't there the previous day. Then more mud, then very nearly the sort of fuck-this-shit mud we had wallowed through the night before, though not quite wet enough to submerge a whole shoe.

Here's a neat thought process you should never start if, like me, you're not a fast ultrarunner:

"Wow, I've been going for 22 hours now."

"If I were fast, I'd be done now."

"I'm not fast."

"How many miles do I have left?"

"Wow, that's a lot. How long will that take me, if I keep going the pace I've been going?"

"Oh wow, that makes me kind of sad."

Instead of doing that, I recommend finding a friend to pace you who cares enough to do things like:

- Take over for the part of your brain that is responsible for self-care and ask every few minutes if you have been eating and drinking, and if everything feels OK
- Make you "run" downhill and flat sections, even if you can't jog faster than 14- or 15-minute miles
- Talk to you even though you're the worst conversation partner ever
- Keep you moving no matter what you say
- Make you eat food at aid stations even when you repeatedly say, "No thanks, I'm fine."
- Put up with all this for 8-12 hours and still be your friend afterward

We trudged onward, thankfully in the shade for most of the morning climbing, leapfrogging with a few people including Katie, a young woman from southern Utah, and her pacer, exchanging wisecracks. The runners of the other Bighorn races, the 50-mile, the 32-mile, and the 18-mile, gradually joined us and shared the trail. Every once in a while, someone would glance over and see my 100-mile bib and offer encouragement or congratulations. At least I think they were looking at my bib to see if I was a 100-mile runner. They may have just assumed by my glacial speed and posture that

I had to be running the 100-mile race.

The hours began to drag, and the pain in my feet and legs kept growing and growing, a steady ache that began as a whisper saying "Stop. Sit Down." It got louder and louder from Mile 70 onward, until it was basically grabbing me by both shoulders, shaking me and yelling, "SIT DOWN." I don't know what other people think about to deal with this kind of thing, but nothing really works for me: not thinking about the food I'm going to eat when I finish, not thinking about seeing my wife, not even thinking about sitting in a chair. Usually I just hike and jog with my mouth hanging slightly open, trying to keep moving as quickly as possible, because there seems to be very little difference in the amount of pain in walking or running this late in the race, and as my friend Brody has kindly pointed out, you might as well shorten the time you're in pain.

Late in my previous two 100-mile races, a similar thing has happened: Around Mile 80 or 85, I encounter another runner who wants to talk about how bad things are. A couple years ago, it was a guy who said he was trying to think about how he could get disqualified so he didn't have to finish the last 20 miles. During my most recent race, it was a guy who was mad that the previous aid station was out of cheese for quesadillas, and that the volunteers told him he was in the home stretch, despite the fact that he had a 5,000-foot climb and a long technical descent remaining.

Thankfully, in the Bighorn 100, this didn't happen. I have a hard enough time keeping the negative thoughts in my own head quiet, let alone trying to drown out

someone else. I mean, nobody's making you do a 100-mile race. What am I supposed to say?
"You're right, Bob, this really is unjust. How dare the forces of the universe conspire to make us do such a painful thing to ourselves." A few days before this, I was listening to a podcast about prison life, and to the stories of men who had done more than a decade in solitary confinement, and how they'd gotten through it. In our situation, in which we volunteered for and paid good money to attempt to find meaning through physical pain, I'm pretty sure we can make it to the finish line despite the lack of cheese, or whatever. (Not that the Bighorn aid stations ran out of cheese, to my knowledge.)

At Mile 87.5, we hit the Upper Sheep Creek aid station, and I grabbed a fistful of bite-sized candy from the tables and ate it while hiking away, with a fervor reminiscent of 9-year-old me on Halloween night. My first Butterfinger in 15 years or so was quite disappointing, but several bite-size Twix bars boosted my morale a little bit. We chugged up our final 500-foot climb, a steep half-mile I had sprinted down the day before, and popped over the top to look into the rolling descent down the Tongue River Canyon, which was larger and longer than I remembered. We jogged a little, but mostly hiked down the steep singletrack. I kept scanning the end of the canyon, looking for a color other than green or brown, an aid station tent that must be just around the corner. I did this for approximately 8,000 downhill steps.

Eventually, a tent and some really nice guys appeared. I negotiated with Jayson for one more five-minute sitting session and had a rather glorious time in a camp chair before we headed out to finish the last 2.2 miles of singletrack.

At the Tongue River Trailhead, our singletrack ended on a dirt road, and the aid station volunteers soaked our arm sleeves and hats with cold water for the sunny final five miles. Apparently someone had tried to drop out of the race earlier at this aid station, five miles from the finish line, and the folks there convinced him to keep going, with a volunteer walking him in.

We walked a lot of the final five miles, me doing the math in my head: If we ran, we'd only cut about 20 minutes off my final time, and I just couldn't motivate to do it. I swear the road was slightly uphill most of the way into town, but that may have been a slight hallucination. We passed a boom box playing the theme from *Chariots of Fire*, and then the theme from *Rocky* (*Rocky II*, I think), and eventually the houses got closer together and we were in town. We jogged the final half-mile into Scott Park, around the perimeter of the park, to the finish line at Mile 100. Jayson was smiling and laughing, and I was just relieved to be done.

 Hilary led us over to a camp chair and some pizza, and we sat for a few minutes and didn't run or walk, finally off the clock after 32.5 hours. It was difficult. But we all signed up for it looking for something difficult, didn't we? I guess I got my money's worth. And hey, a free belt buckle.

13

WE ARE RUNNING NOWHERE

My dad used to love this old Rodney Dangerfield joke that went something like this: "My old man, I told him I'm tired of running around in circles. So he nailed my other foot to the floor." I guess I do not share Rodney Dangerfield's disdain for going around in circles.

--

Here's a strange thing I did a couple weeks ago: I left my house in running clothes, with a couple packages and envelopes in my hand, and ran to the nearest post office a couple miles away. I walked in, dropped the packages off, walked back out, and ran another four miles before I went home. Very simple, but I felt like a genius, sort of multitasking exercise with an office task, killing two birds with one stone, insert dad joke about "running errands" here.

I do this every once in a while: I actually run somewhere to do something besides just run. The post office, the ATM, or the grocery store to pick up one thing I can carry home in my hand. But most of the time, like probably everybody else who runs, I run nowhere.

I start and stop my runs at the same place: My house, or my car parked at a trailhead. I run around for hours, sometimes in circles, and when I finish, I have burned hundreds or thousands of calories, and I end up exactly where I've started, except the sun has moved several degrees across the sky and the temperature has changed. A few weeks ago, I did a long run around the park near my house, eight laps, passing the same group of people sitting in the grass, who were taking turns standing up holding a cardboard sign asking passing motorists for change and/or food. Lots of people would say I was being "productive" and they were not, but every time I passed, I thought, "Those people must think I am a complete idiot, and they are right. It's 89 degrees out here." In the time I spent running, they probably made a few dollars. I made zero dollars. If you factor in the energy blocks I ate while running and the depreciation of my running shoes, I actually lost money on the whole thing.

When I got home from my run, my dog greeted me, tail wagging, and, being a dog, was unsure if I had been gone for 30 minutes or four and a half hours, or if I had run three miles or 26 miles. To my dog, and really, to the rest of the society I live in, it really didn't matter much if I had run at all. For all my dog knew, I could have been spreading mulch in the front yard for 20 minutes before I came in the door, or maybe just standing out there thinking about taking him for his next walk. To him, and really, in the grand scheme of things, I hadn't gone anywhere at all.

I am not a nihilist, I don't think. To me, there's a point to all this running, or at least a few benefits, like the ability to eat more pizza and not gain (too much) weight, and spending chunks of time purposely *not* looking at a computer or phone screen. But you have to admit, it's a lot of travel. According to my Strava log, with all the miles I've run nowhere this year, I could have left my house in Denver on January 1 and I'd almost be to Washington D.C. right now. But here I am, standing at my house.

I use an app to keep track, via a complex satellite communication system, how much I've run nowhere every time I go out. I do this to keep track how prepared (or unprepared) I will be for my next race, an event in which I will get together with dozens or thousands of people to run nowhere, theoretically as fast as we can.

All these runners, as well as millions of people around the world, make running nowhere a priority in their lives. In order to make time for running, most of us take steps to make the rest of our lives efficient: shortcuts, techniques, apps, and inventions that ensure we will have a few hours per week free so we can run around instead of, say, making bread from scratch or chopping firewood. And then we run, not to get from Point A to Point B, but from Point A back to Point A.

Objectively, we have traveled nowhere. But I continue to run, because I still feel like I'm getting somewhere.

14

MARATHON TIPS FROM MY FRIEND SYD

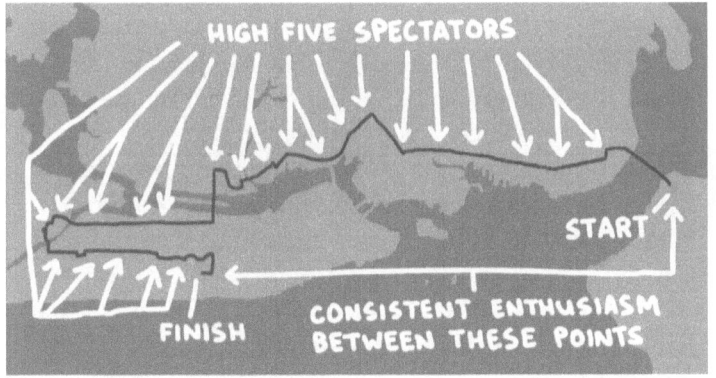

I ran the New York City Marathon for the first time in 2019, and I wanted to write something about the experience, but I wasn't really sure how to go about it. I hadn't really taken mile-by-mile mental notes—I was just running around with my friend Syd, being a tourist and having fun with it. It's hard to write something that captures some sort of universal experience of a particular race (and maybe not a good idea to try, especially when it's your first time at that race?). But I thought, hey, I'm an expert at what it was like to run the race with Syd, who I think does a pretty good job of having a great time. So I tried that angle.

--

These tips are entirely based on my observations while running the 2019 NYC Marathon with Syd, his 11th time running the race. He is not a professional runner, but has a pretty good track record at finishing marathons, and is generally a ray of sunshine.

IN THE MONTHS BEFORE THE MARATHON
Train by running a lot.

IN THE HOURS BEFORE THE MARATHON
Make sure you go No. 2. Going No. 2 before the race will shave anywhere from two minutes to eight minutes off your marathon time by preventing you from having to stop mid-run at a port-a-potty to go No. 2, and potentially wait in line for several minutes at said port-a-potty.

Bring enough snacks to eat so you're not hungry when you start running.

WHILE WAITING FOR THE MARATHON TO START
Wear a black trash bag with a hole cut for your head. This will keep you warm, as well as give you privacy if you need to apply Body Glide to sensitive regions and/or take a last-minute pee in an emptied Gatorade bottle (which you have also brought along).

AFTER THE MARATHON STARTS
Run 26.2 miles without quitting.

Cheer back at spectators who yell words of

encouragement in your direction, with the goal of pumping them up as much as they pump you up, if not more.

Stop, and even run backwards, to help other runners up if they trip and fall.

Avoid pooping your pants at all costs.

No matter how tired you are, summon the energy for dozens of genuine smiles.

Hug your wife, mother, and father, and anyone else who has come out to cheer specifically for you along the race course.

Every once in a while, yell YEAH at no one or everyone.

Thank all aid station volunteers.

High-five kids.

High-five all signs that say "Push here for power boost" or similar.

Generally focus on being grateful you can run 26.2 miles and if the weather is nice, be grateful for that, too.

When encountering race photographers, give no indication that you have been running for one, two, or three hours, and give them a pose and smile worthy of printing in next year's marathon marketing materials and/or signage.

Pump one or more fists when running past live bands and DJs.

Suppress all complaints and other negative verbal statements until the end of the race.

Run your fastest two miles from Mile 24.2 to the finish line.

AT THE FINISH LINE OF THE MARATHON
Congratulate people around you even if they are complete strangers you have never seen before and will never see again.

AFTER THE RACE
Use pizza to replace all the calories you burned while running, and use additional pizza as necessary.

Talk about maybe not running a marathon next year, but leave it open so you can maybe talk yourself into running another marathon next year.

15

HOW TO GO FOR A RUN IN 22 SIMPLE STEPS

I do a great job of procrastinating my runs. Do I take steps to learn to stop procrastinating them? No I do not. I do, however, spend time finding new ways to joke about said procrastination. This particular joke got pretty elaborate, but it's not like I'm making this stuff up—I literally have done every single one of these things. Except I've never had a Tinder account (I just threw that in to make #3 more universally relevant).

--

1. Congratulations, you've decided to go for a run. Today. As you probably know, that's the first step towards going for a run, so pat yourself on the back for that. But hold on—there are a few more things you need to do before you head out the door and take that real first stride of your run, however long it may be.

2. First things first: Get dressed for your run. What's the weather like out there? Sure, you could open a window or a door and get a feel for the temperature, but for the most reliable, up-to-the-minute forecast, you should probably check a weather app on your phone.

3. After you've seen the weather forecast, you might as well cycle through all the apps you usually check eight to 40 times every day, just to make sure you won't be missing anything while you're out there running: email, text messages, Instagram, Twitter, Strava, Zillow, PetFinder, your bank account, Nest, Tinder.

4. Now you're ready to get dressed appropriately for the weather. Find your stuff and put it on. Except where's your favorite running hat? Not where you usually put it. Find that hat. Sure, you could go for a run without it, but why would you?

5. While looking for your hat, which could take two to 25 minutes, have a snack just to make sure you don't bonk out there. You don't have to prepare anything elaborate, just something quick. But, also, you could prepare something a little more elaborate. Either way, get some calories in you.

6. While ingesting said calories, pick up a magazine and read an article. Or two. Doesn't have to be about running.

7. Do you need to carry a water bottle on today's run? Find the bottle, but not the lid.

8. Dig around in the cupboard until you find the lid to your water bottle.

9. The nozzle looks a little funky, doesn't it? Might as well scrub it clean now, because you know you won't feel like doing it after your run.

10. Fill up your now-clean water bottle.

11. Find your hat. Or don't find it. Decide to do some stretches.

12. Actually, before you do those stretches, do a little warm up. Get those hips loosened up, maybe a couple squats, lunges, a couple pushups, just so you're not stretching cold muscles.

13. Do some stretches. You really should have a more strategic stretch routine, don't you think? Grab your phone and google "stretches for runners." Check out four or five different ones before deciding on one. Also read a few news articles before you start stretching.

14. Do all the stretches. Feels good, doesn't it? Now you're ready.

15. Actually, better use the bathroom one more time before you head out. You never know.

16. Check your phone apps one more time, just in case you've missed anything while getting dressed, eating, reading that magazine article, warming up and stretching.

17. You're ready for your run! Head out the door!

18. Now that you're actually outside, it feels a lot cooler or warmer than your weather app said it was supposed to be. Head back inside to shed a layer or add a layer.

19. OK, now you're ready. Put in your earbuds so

you'll have some music to run to.

20. But all these playlists and albums are getting boring. Create a new playlist that will be the perfect length for today's run. Walk back inside so your phone will connect to wifi.

21. OK, now you're really ready for your run! Except wow, it seems like it's going to get dark soon. Maybe you should take a headlamp or a small flashlight? Yeah, head back inside and grab one, just in case.

22. Press play on that playlist, and begin running. Think about how running is great because it's so simple and easy, because all you need to do is lace up your shoes and head out the door, just like that.

16

52 MARATHONS IN A YEAR

If you're reading the essays in this book in order, you should know: This entire year of marathons was inspired by our New York Pizza Marathon (Chapter 7), which was not fast, nor a real race, but 26.2 miles, and fun. It got me to thinking that a bunch of marathons might be kind of fun. Spoiler: A bunch of marathons was kind of fun. Kind of. Sometimes. Occasionally, anyway.

--

In 2019, I set out to run 52 marathons in 52 weeks. When I started on January 2, running down snow-covered dirt roads near my parents' house in central Iowa, I hadn't come up with a solid reason why—I just figured I'd run 26.2 miles and see how it went. If it went well, I'd run 26.2 miles the next week too, and if that went well, I'd keep going. I had only told a couple people, including my wife, Hilary, and I hadn't exactly used committed language when I said it out loud: "*I think I might try to* run 52 marathons in 52 weeks this year *and see how it goes*."

The first one went fine: It was 21 degrees Fahrenheit outside when I started, with the chilly Iowa winter humidity hanging in the air, and a low-angle January sun lighting the bare cornfields. I saw a handful of cars, got chased by a dog down a dirt road, but not bitten, and when I finished in 4 hours and 20 minutes, I didn't feel horrible. That was a Wednesday. I certainly didn't feel like I could run a marathon the next morning, but maybe in a few days.

The following Monday, January 7, I ran another marathon, mostly on bike paths near my parents' house, 4:14:36 this time. A little pain on the outside of my left knee, but nothing major. Mostly I felt good knocking out two marathons in the first seven days of the year. I figured it was better to get ahead of the one-per-week pace early in the year, in case I got sick or had a minor injury and had to take time off later. Plus, I'd rather get the running in cold weather out of the way on the front end than have to cram in five or six marathons in December.

It didn't feel like that crazy of a thing to be doing—I had watched the film about Dean Karnazes's 50 marathons in 50 states in 50 days back in 2008, and although he's a super-athlete, I remember thinking that he just made it feel so doable. And if he could do it in 50 days with no rest days in between, certainly I could do 52 marathons with 6 days to rest in between each one, right?

I'm certainly not the first person to do something like this—if you search the internet, you'll find quite a few people who have done it, and far crazier things:

- American Jay Helgerson was the first to do it in 1980

- Canadian Terry Fox, who had his leg amputated because of osteosarcoma, ran 143 marathons in 143 days on a prosthetic leg to raise awareness about cancer, in 1980
- American Karl Gruber did it in 1996 and 1997 (and wrote a how-to book about it)
- Dane Rauschenberg ram 52 marathons in 52 weeks in 2006
- Dean Karnazes ran the aforementioned 50 marathons in 50 states in 50 days in 2006 (and wrote a book about it)(and made a movie)
- Australian Tristan Miller did 52 marathons in 42 countries in 2010 (and wrote a book about it)
- Irishman Aiden Sheridan ran 59 marathons in 2016 to raise money for breast cancer
- American Julie Weiss did it in 2012 and 2013 to raise money for pancreatic cancer research
- Belgian Stefaan Engels ran 365 marathons in 365 days in 2011
- Alan Murray and Janette Murray-Wakelin ran 366 marathons in 366 days in Australia in 2013
- Comedian Eddie Izzard ran 27 marathons in 27 days in 2016 to raise money for the UK charity Sport Relief
- Michael Ortiz ran 52 100-mile races in a year
- Walter Handloser ran 50 100-mile races in 2019

I had decided to do 52 26.2-mile runs—not races—in 52 weeks. Most of the time people do something like this, as far as my research showed, they run races, which is a completely different thing when you account for all the scheduling, logistics, and travel. I just wanted to do the running, so I did what I called "Strava marathons." I started my watch, started running, and stopped when my watch said 26.2 miles.

At the beginning of the year, I planned on signing up for at least one ultramarathon, the Bighorn 100 in Wyoming in June. Training for a 100-mile race involves so many training runs that are pretty near marathon distance, so I thought running a marathon a week leading up to the Bighorn wouldn't be that off-base, training-wise.

I had also planned to pace my friend Forest in the Hellbender 100 in North Carolina in early April. He got injured, and I half-jokingly suggested I could step in for him, and of course a half-joke always has a 50 percent chance of being taken seriously, so a month before the race, I found myself signed up to crank out 100 miles with 24,000 feet of elevation gain in the Black Mountains. I mentioned to Forest my 52 Marathons plan, saying that I thought I might just count a 100-mile race as one marathon. He said that was a terrible idea, so I changed my mind and decided to count a 100-mile race as three marathons. At the start of the race, I would start my Strava app on my phone, pull out my phone when I got close to 26.2 miles and check it, wait for it to roll over 26.2 miles, stop it, save it, and start another Strava activity. I'm sure a few people would say that's not truly running 52 marathons in a year, and if that's your opinion, I would invite you to do 52 marathons in a year in whatever style you decide is pure and just.

Another friend said I should extend my 100-mile races a few miles so I could get four marathons out of them, instead of three marathons and a 21.4-mile run. I told him that was a terrible idea, and that I was not interested in doing it. However, at the finish line of the Bighorn 100, I did have some regret when I checked my phone at the end of the race and saw that I was only 5.5 miles from finishing a fourth marathon. But, Hilary had brought pizza and a camp chair to the finish line, so that was the end of that.

--

They were all the same distance, 26.2 miles, but some of them felt like completely opposite ends of the spectrum. I ran my fastest time in just under 3 hours and 48 minutes on #48, in the mostly-flat City Park near my house (only 566 feet of elevation gain), and the slowest one was almost 13 hours, helping my friend Dave to the top of his first 14er ever, Longs Peak, in August, and tacking on a few more miles up the nearby Estes Cone afterward (7,746 feet of elevation gain).

I did most of the marathons alone, but the only time I really felt "lonely" was during Marathon #17, around Mile 62 of the Hellbender 100, jogging along through the forest around 1:30 a.m. over a path covered in fallen leaves. I realized I hadn't seen a headlamp, a light from a house or a car, or any human beings for about an hour. There were only 75 people in the race, and I'd found a pocket somewhere in the eight miles between aid stations where I was totally by myself for quite a while, running in a small bubble of light illuminated by my headlamp, set on its low setting to preserve the battery. There was no wind in the stand of trees, and it was dead silent, to the point where if a racoon had rustled some leaves 50 feet away, I probably would have heard it. I literally thought to myself, "if this were a horror movie, it would be a perfect spot for someone to come flying at me from the right or left with an axe/chainsaw/sword," and then quickly thought, "STOP doing that, it is not helpful." About 20 minutes later, I finally saw the lights of the next aid station, at Mile 65.

The New York City Marathon was on the complete opposite end of the spectrum, starting on a chilly fall morning in Staten Island from a temporary village of 53,000 other runners. It was a bizarre gathering, like some sort of weird music festival with all the dry plain bagels, bananas, and Honey Stinger waffles you could eat, but that you should maybe bring your own toilet paper to if you planned on using one of the hundreds of very popular port-a-potties. Anyone who's run it can tell you about the masses of incredible people that line the streets of Brooklyn, Queens, the Bronx, and Manhattan from about Mile 3 to Mile 26, cheering encouragement, and, as I found out, many of whom hand out Fun Size candy bars, which are incredibly satisfying. It was a long way from plodding along in the woods alone, trying to stay motivated and also not go crazy in the middle of the night.

Most of the runs, however, I did by myself, near my home in Denver. I ran 16 marathons right out my front door, sometimes taking my dog for the first few miles and then dropping him off back at the house, turning around and running the last 20-some miles. I ran another 10 marathons on the trails and dirt roads at William Frederick Hayden Park (aka Green Mountain) in Lakewood, 25 minutes from where I live, and another 12 in other places in Colorado's Front Range within a 90-minute drive from our house. All the miles in the city, and all those miles at Green Mountain, sort of blurred together by halfway through the summer. I had thought maybe I'd take notes after each marathon, describe the weather and how I was feeling, write what

I thought about while running, or what I saw, but lots of them weren't that notable. Not that I expected they would all be amazing experiences when I started doing them.

The year started cold as I ran every week, remembering to enjoy the cool weather through spring before it got hot. In Denver some years, it seems like summer lasts six months. On July 15th, I ran the hottest marathon all year (#30), when the temperature got up to 95 degrees by the end of my run. I'm not good at exercising in the heat, but I am even worse at convincing myself to get out of bed early to avoid the heat, so I just trudged it out, taking several short breaks to walk parts of the final six miles.

Eleven days later, on July 26th, the temperature got up to 89 degrees during my marathon (#32), and for the last five miles, I fantasized about the beverage cooler at the 7-Eleven near my house. After I turned out of the park for the final mile or so home, I started zig-zagging on a few blocks in order to end my run at 7-Eleven at 26.2 miles, walked in, and got the first Big Gulp of Coca-Cola I've had in maybe a decade. I walked home sipping it, drenched in sweat with salt marks appearing everywhere the sweat had dried, and I would be surprised if anyone on Earth was enjoying a soda as much as I was for those five minutes.

I didn't even think to look up the dictionary definition of a marathon until late in the year, well into the project, and despite consulting a few different dictionaries, every definition I found used the word "race." So I suppose if you wanted to be strict about it, you could say I wasn't really running 52 marathons, just 52 marathon-length runs. Despite this semantic issue, I decided to finish the project.

--

As fall came, the temperature started to cool a little bit, and the idea of completing the whole mission started to seem possible, but definitely not a sure thing. I had experienced some pain in my knee for a while at the beginning of the year, but it didn't get worse, so I just kept going and it eventually went away. The same thing happened with a weird pain in my left foot near my ankle that lasted from late August through mid-October (but never got any worse). While crossing some of the busy streets near City Park in Denver during my last three or four marathons, I definitely worried about the possibility of getting hit by a car during Marathon #50 or #51, so close to the end—or, after a snowstorm in November, slipping on some ice and injuring myself. Thankfully, none of those things ever happened.

As the temperatures got colder and I got into the last five marathons, and could sort of see the metaphorical finish line, I thought about making a big deal of the last one, maybe inviting a bunch of friends to join me, turn it into a little bit of a celebration. Then I started thinking about the date, where we'd run, running with eight or 10 people, what if someone needed to stop and use the bathroom, lining all of it up, and I realized that planning something would be a lot of work. I thought about why I was doing it, something I never really established, besides the fact that I turned 40 this year. I wasn't doing it to raise money or raise awareness for anything (although I respect the people who have done similar things to raise money or awareness for causes), or really to inspire anyone to do the same thing. More than once, I thought about how ridiculous it was, even if I rationalized it by saying that lots of people go to the gym three times a week for 90 minutes—this was just the equivalent of doing all those gym sessions in one day. Maybe it would be cool if it inspired someone to run a 10K every weekend for a year, or even walk a 10K every weekend for a year. For themselves, or for a good cause, whatever.

--

I decided to do Marathon #52 by myself. I ran #51 on a Monday, December 2nd, in the snow and slush, when it was 50 degrees and sunny, and before I was even done with it, I just wanted to hurry up and get #52 over with. I thought about just filling my water bottles and heading back out on a second marathon, but thought better. A couple days' rest would be good. Thursday or Friday I could do the last one. The weather forecast for Thursday was not ideal, 80 percent chance of rain, then snow, high of 41 degrees. I went to bed Wednesday night thinking I'd see how it looked in the morning and decide then.

On Thursday, the rain started at 8:40 a.m., and kept up until about noon, and after it let up, I told Hilary, I think I'm just going to go for it. I ate a quick bowl of oatmeal, filled my water bottles, stuffed them in my vest, and headed out the door. It was perfect, if by "perfect," you mean "shitty conditions totally appropriate to cap a year of making yourself do things when you didn't really feel like it": cold, humid, cloudy, wet roads and sidewalks, clumps of dirty snow and ice hanging around. Around mile 9, it started drizzling again. This was exactly how the last one should go: lonely, and fairly miserable.

I had a moment, about mile 24.7 of 26.2, during the final two miles of the final marathon of the year, running in the dark under streetlights, finally finding a bit of a stride after slogging out six or seven slow, low-morale miles. It was cold, it had been drizzling rain for almost three hours, but I wasn't cold at all—I felt like a machine, just rolling along, oblivious to the weather and my own fatigue. It reminded me a little bit of a scene in a movie. Except in the movie, the runner would be training for something—something daunting, terrifying, some sort of test that would be the narrative climax of the movie. I wasn't training for anything. I was just doing what I'd been doing every week. This was the thing, the miles and miles of being outside, by myself, moving. There was no Great Sports Contest coming up, just hopefully more running, just like this, for as long as I can keep doing it.

Other notes:

- I did run several actual marathon races: The Colfax Marathon in Denver (Marathon #22), the Missoula Marathon (Marathon #28), the NYC Marathon (Marathon #47).
- The ultramarathons I ran were: The Hellbender 100 (Marathons #15, #16, and #17), The Bighorn 100 (Marathons #25, #26, and #27), the Bear Chase Trail Race 50K (Marathon #42), and the Mines of Spain 100K (Marathons #45 and #46).

- At one point in March, I needed to do a bunch of elevation gain to train for the Hellbender 100, and I needed to do a 50-mile run, but in March, not many steep trails are snow-free in the Denver area. So my best option, I felt, was to do my training run on a dirt road going to the top of Green Mountain, which was dry enough. If you go from the west parking lot over the top of the mountain to a set of radio towers, it's 2.0 miles and 850 feet of elevation gain. So I ran back and forth on that road until I got to two marathons that day, totaling 53 miles and 12,272 feet of elevation gain, on one two-mile stretch of road.
- I did a similar training day in May, same location, with more dry trails, 52.6 miles and 9,861 feet of elevation gain.
- I live in Denver, which has pretty mild weather most of the year.
- I'm self-employed, which means I can juggle my schedule to accommodate bad weather. For example, if the weather is going to be terrible on Saturday, I can usually take Friday off to run and do all my work on Saturday instead.
- I also don't have kids, which of course makes something like this a lot easier.
- I ran mostly by myself, but had friends join me for parts or all of several marathons: Hilary Oliver (parts of #3, #14, and #18, all of #22, #28, and #42), Jayson Sime (all of #12, parts of #6, #10, #19, #27, #33, #40), Forest Woodward (part of #16, all of #6, #45, and #46), Dave Fecik (parts of #34, #35, and #46), Syd Jones (all of #47), and Ryan Van Duzer (all of #49).
- I wore a hydration vest for all but two of the marathons—the Colfax Marathon, and the NYC

Marathon (which doesn't allow vests with pockets). I did this so I could carry all of my water and food and not have to return to my house or car, where I find it very easy to lose motivation to continue running. The most water I ever started a day with was about 80 ounces, in two soft bottles and a 50-ounce hydration reservoir.
- The coldest one was Marathon #1, on dirt roads near my parents' house in Iowa, 21 degrees, Jan. 2nd
- The warmest temperature was 95 degrees, in Denver, on July 15th (Marathon #30)
- Longest break between marathons was: 15 days, 12 hours (between Marathon #46 and #47)
- Shortest break between marathons (that weren't on the same day) was 67 hours, 41 minutes, between Marathon #8 and Marathon #9)
- By state, here's where I ran:
  - Colorado: 38 marathons
  - Iowa: 4 marathons
  - Wyoming: 3 marathons
  - Utah: 1 marathon
  - Montana: 2 marathons
  - New York: 1 marathon
  - North Carolina: 3 marathons

17

WINTER RUNNING TIPS FOR MASOCHISTS

*In 2017, someone told me about an episode of Malcolm Gladwell's Revisionist History podcast called "The Satire Paradox," in which Gladwell makes the point that while satire is funny, it's really ineffective at changing anyone's mind about anything. Which was a revolutionary idea to me, because I have definitely enjoyed satire throughout my life—*Catch 22 *blew my mind when I read it the year after I got out of college, and* The Onion *has always been a huge influence. The idea that making fun of people doesn't change their minds seems obvious, when you put it that way, so I really shouldn't have been surprised. But the more I thought about it, the more it aligned with a feeling I'd had as I'd learned to write online: Making fun of a group of people is kind of fun, but only until you realize you've hurt someone's feelings. Then it kind of sucks. But there's one person whose feelings never get hurt, no matter how much I poke fun at them: Me.*

So I made a rule: <u>Making fun of "them" = Not OK.</u> <u>Making fun of "us" = OK.</u> As long as I could include *myself in a group, that group was fair game. As a runner, I do some dumb shit. And if I do it, there's a chance that some other runner out there does it too, and if I make fun of it, maybe we can come together a little bit, as the goofballs that we are. That's where pieces like this one come from.*

--

Winter is the prime season for lots of fun activities: skiing, snowboarding, ice climbing, ice skating, curling, and sledding among them. But you'd rather not have fun. You'd rather keep running through the worst weather of the year—getting wet, getting cold. Having your extremities go numb from cold and then electric with shooting pains when rewarmed, snot freezing inside your nose, breathing heavily in air so cold you wonder if you're doing permanent damage to your respiratory system, in constant fear of ripping knee ligaments from a hard slip on some ice. No one but you knows why you do it, but that's OK, you fucking weirdo. To keep you running through the dark, cold, miserable, lonely, demoralizing, uncomfortable, and hopeless, season that is winter, and to keep you as miserable, cold, and demoralized as possible while doing it, here are a few tips:

1. First of all, stick with running, outdoors, even though you have heard of many reasonable cold-weather alternatives such as Nordic skiing, snowshoeing, spin

classes, treadmills, and staying under a blanket eating pizza rolls.

2. Do not wear gloves or mittens, or even long sleeves, unless the air temperature is in single digits.

3. When wearing gloves, wear only very thin gloves. As you head out the door, say to yourself, "These should be fine," even though in your heart, you know they are not sufficient at all.

4. Avoid daylight as much as possible. Procrastinate your weekend runs so that they take place not in the middle of the day, when the temperature is the warmest, but in the cold, lonely, hopeless dark of night.

5. Wear cotton for all your layers, but especially next to your skin to maximize retention of sweat moisture, which will then freeze. Overdressing in too many layers will enable you to sweat more, ensuring a good sweat-freeze a few minutes into your run.

6. Buy some microspikes. Wear them when you do not need them, i.e. you see snow on the ground but your running route is 95 percent snow-free, so you just end up grinding down your metal traction devices on pavement or asphalt and sort of cringing the entire time, and only occasionally making contact with a small patch of snow or ice you probably could have stepped around, but what the hell, you're wearing microspikes.

7. When conditions are actually sketchy enough to justify traction devices, i.e. lots of ice and snow everywhere, and ice covered by snow, do not wear those microspikes. Talk yourself out of it, proclaim as you leave the house, "It doesn't look too bad out there," and then confidently stride away, making sharp turns whenever possible.

8. If you slip on ice and start to fall, try to break your fall with your elbows, tailbone, kneecaps, or, if you're really going for it, your face.

9. Carry a leaky water bottle with you at all times to keep one or both of your hands soaking wet as you run.

10. When it snows, find a running route where you can maximize postholing. Ideally, you will be able to find a trailhead where everyone else is wearing snowshoes—that's a good sign that the snow is deep and soft enough that it's impossible to enjoy it without flotation, and that it will be prime for miles of postholing shin-deep, or if it's your lucky day, crotch-deep.

11. If possible, find a route that runs next to spots where large puddles of dirty slush form, so you can maximize your exposure to sudden cold, wet, nasty showers of melted precipitation mixed with street runoff when cars drive through them and send the crud flying.

12. On that route with all the street puddles, time your runs with the city transit schedule so you can enjoy being hit in the face by splashes from buses. Run with your mouth open.

13. When you reach a point when you feel it's just too horrible, when you're exhausted from postholing, soaked from a city bus splashing you with brown slush, and your hands are numb, and you're so cold you're seriously thinking about peeing your pants just for a few seconds of fleeting warmth: Cry. Don't stop running, but go ahead and cry. It's OK. Let those tears flow, until they freeze to your cheeks as you plod along, only to be melted by more tears. And then tell yourself: "I am crying because I just love running in the winter so much."

18

THE YEAR OF MAKING YOUR OWN FUN RUN

After a few summers of learning how to train for long races, 2020 unfolded, well, the way it did, and I didn't really have a big goal to train for. But I kept running anyway, and I started to realize that the "training runs" I did, long days out on the trail in order to "prepare" for some future organized event, were actually themselves kind of the whole point. So I started dreaming up a big loop, starting and ending at the edge of town.

--

The realization did not come at one exact moment, but as a sort of a slow admission over a few hours on the trail: I had vastly underestimated the whole thing. I'd look up at the angle of the sun through the trees, glance at my watch, do a little math in my head trying to estimate the miles I had left and the approximate time of the sunset, and panic a little bit.

Like a fool, I had "figured" I'd be running and hiking maybe two hours in the dark to the trailhead at the end. This was somewhat based on very rough math, but mostly on optimism. By 5:00 p.m., I had been moving for nine hours, had gotten through 35 miles and the majority of the elevation gain, and was feeling pretty good overall.

I came to a fork in the trail, with two options: go left, to 25-30 more miles of trail with only two hours of daylight remaining, or go right, to a trailhead eight miles away, where I could call for a ride, get picked up before dark, grab a pizza, take a shower, put my feet up, and flop into a warm, comfortable bed at a decent hour.

There were no more good bail spots if I went left, so I'd be committed to the whole thing, making the total day about 60 miles and 12,000 feet of climbing, summiting five peaks. I was tired, unsure if I'd find any water sources in the last 25 miles, and really not physically prepared for it. But jeez, if I bailed, I'd have to come back and do the whole thing over next year. The whole thing being this arguably contrived loop of trails that I'd drawn on a map, a project I'd made up and decided I wanted to try, that no one besides me cared if I completed.

I went left.

I've thought a lot about what we'll remember about 2020 when we look back on it a decade from now. It's unquestionably been a weird year for many of us, a very tough year for many of us, and probably more than any other year in the past several decades, it has required that we all adjust our lives in not insignificant ways. Working from home, having our kids trying to go to school from home, trying to work from home while having our kids try to go to school from home, wearing masks in public spaces, finding new ways to socialize with friends and family, not visiting restaurants, the list goes on and on—and in 2020, I think the one thing we've all had to do is get creative, and adapt.

If you were a person who built at least part of their year around races—something that seems in retrospect both incredibly privileged and a relic of a long-ago life—it was clear that for a few months, or maybe a year, you were going to have to find a way to make your own fun. People started running marathons around their block, marathons in their apartments, ultramarathons on treadmills in their apartments—a guy in Japan ran 100 miles on a single 15-meter trail around a tree, 10,667 laps.

For me, running at all felt like a luxury. After a huge running year in 2019, I ran a 50K race on January 25th, then promptly got a cold, which turned into a chronic (non-Covid) cough. I went two months without running a single step while I tried to figure out what was causing the cough. Eventually, we worked it out that yes, running was OK, and on March 25th, just after our Covid lockdowns were beginning, I was able to run two miles in my neighborhood, crossing the street to avoid getting too close to anyone on the sidewalk, and wearing a buff around my neck just in case. I reminded myself how fortunate I was to be able to move outdoors at all, and breathe freely.

Eventually I was able to run five miles, then six, then eight, and I decided to try to run every street in my neighborhood, which took a lot longer than I figured. Then I started venturing to the park a mile from our house and running around the crushed gravel path there, giving a wide berth to anyone else I passed in either direction. In mid-May, I tentatively drove out to a trailhead to see how things went, wondering if it would be possible to stay six feet away from people on singletrack (it was).

I'd canceled all my race plans for the year, and all my travel plans, and arrived very quickly at a place where I was happy to still have a job and relatively good health. I read someone's tweet telling people that this was just a pause, not a full stop, and reminded myself of that. I adjusted expectations, and figured if I got to go on a handful of trail runs over the next year, that was still pretty fantastic.

We moved to a new state in July, and had new trails to explore, right at the edge of town. I bought local maps, downloaded apps on my phone, and tried to schedule my trail runs to coincide with less-busy times to avoid other people.

As I got back in shape and increased the mileage of my runs, the running world started talking about 2020 being the "Year of the FKT," or Fastest Known Time. Elite runners, with no races to compete in, started trying to beat fastest known times on objectives like Nolan's 14 in Colorado, the Wonderland Trail around Mt. Rainier, and the Ice Age Trail in Wisconsin. NPR did a story on FKTs, then *Men's Journal* did a story on them, then NPR did another one.

I am not what you might call an FKT kind of guy, but I had browsed the Fastest Known Time website, and what struck a chord with me were the people who submitted routes that weren't necessarily going to attract the attention of, say, world-class ultrarunners, but were creative. Someone traversed the entire Mojave National Preserve, from the middle of nowhere to the middle of nowhere. Someone else has the FKT for running between all three lighthouses on Nantucket Island. Someone else submitted an FKT of a run that stops at all the PATH train stations in New Jersey and New York (and includes a train ride across the Hudson River).

Yes, it's a website about people doing human-powered things as fast as they can, but to me, it's also a site where people create fun things for other people to read about and/or do. In 2020, the Fastest Known Time website went over the 3,000-route mark.

What if, I thought, I could put together a big route that other people could try to do? The first time I did it would be the FKT, but then maybe it'd be interesting enough that other (faster) people would go for it. That would be fun. Or at least "fun," you know, in quotes, not fun during, fun later.

I sat in our temporary apartment a few late summer nights, looking at maps of the Rattlesnake National Recreation Area, running my finger around the trails, looking for a line that made sense. I started tracing a route on CalTopo.com, going over the tops of peaks, trying to piece it together.

By the end of August, I had it: A loop around the Rattlesnake, summiting five peaks, almost completely on trails. According to my mouse-click mapping, it would be right around 60 miles and 12,000 feet of elevation gain. I had been running enough mileage and doing enough uphill that I was in pretty good shape for it. I was ready.

And then, we had a really bad week of wildfire smoke, so I didn't do it. And I didn't do any running, playing it safe with the awful air quality and having spent the first half of the year with that chronic cough. And then we moved into a new house, and then I left to teach a writing workshop. My weekly running mileage fell off a cliff and my calorie consumption did not, but the Rattlesnake Loop was still in the back of my mind.

In early October, I thought, what the hell, I might as well give it a shot. Snow would be falling up high in the next week or two, and once that happened, I might as well wait until next year
.
As my friend Alan said to me once, "People show up rested or ready. We'll be rested."

I parked a car at the trailhead where I'd end the loop and got out in the chilly morning air, hoping to be hopping back into the driver's seat not too much later that evening. It was 43 degrees, and I was in shorts, a short-sleeved t-shirt and a wind jacket. I pulled the hood up, grabbed my running vest out of the back of the car, and at the last second looked at the thin pair of running gloves I'd brough. Nah, I don't need these, I thought, glancing up at the sun and then tossing the gloves back in the car.

I started my watch and ran a few blocks across the neighborhood, to the first section of trail. The plan was to stay as high as possible and loop around the entire Rattlesnake Creek drainage on trails for all but about a half-mile, tagging the summits of Stuart Peak (7,791 ft), Mosquito Peak (8,057 feet), Mineral Peak (7,447 feet), Sheep Mountain (7,646 feet), and Mt. Jumbo (4,546 feet), and then descend the last couple miles of trail to my car. The plan was also: to run as much as I could, feel good doing it, not run out of water or food, not experience any chafing or blisters, keep morale high, and not quit early.

I jogged past a few people out for a morning hike or a morning dog walk, a mountain biker, and then started a sustained climb. It was a beautiful fall morning, with leaves turning amber, the sun low enough in the sky to color everything a bit golden, and crisp air. At the Snowbowl Overlook, around Mile 12 at just before 11 a.m., I passed by a mountain biker who had stopped to take a photo. He said, "You're crushing it," and I said thanks. He would be the last human being I'd see the entire day.

A friend of mine said to me a long time ago that you basically have two options when you do things for fun: you can find things that other people have made up and do those for fun, or you can make your own fun. This was, if I remember correctly, while a group of us were biking 10 or 12 miles to a place that served a burrito called "The Gut Buster," which we would all eat and then pedal back home. We assumed at least one of us would vomit, thus making it the "Gut Buster Triathlon" (bike + eat burrito + regurgitate burrito). This was a fun thing we had made up to do on a Friday night. Two other friends had bailed at the last minute to go to a concert, a thing other people had made up.

I am a fan of both making up my own fun things as well

as doing other things people have made up, but I have to say, when you're making up your own fun, the ideation process and the planning are probably half of the enjoyment for me. Maybe you're talking to a friend and you say, "we should do that, but on bikes instead," or "how many donut shops are in the whole city?" and then "think we could run between all of them in one day?" or "what about trying to go from Point A to, hear me out … Point C?"

Your idea of fun is your idea of fun. There are no rules. You just make something up and do it, and if other people hear about it, they either think it sounds fun, or not fun. And maybe they do it themselves someday. I think about all the things we do that are accepted as fun—at the beginning, they were probably all met with some skepticism. Like running 100 miles all at once, or standup paddleboarding, or eating really spicy food. They're all contrived ideas someone had, and shared with other people, to some level of success.

At some point, someone made up the idea of playing poker, and other people probably had a lot of questions:

"OK, so three of these is better than two of those?"

"The ones with the faces are more valuable then?"

"Why don't we each get six cards?"

"OK, and now I give you all my money and now I don't have enough money to pay rent next month?"

I have made up things to do for decades, from watching all the *Godfather* movies in one day, to running a marathon around New York and eating a slice of pizza every five miles, to bicycling the entire length of Colfax Avenue in Denver, to hiking the "Seven Summits" of the city of Phoenix in one day. I cannot more highly recommend making your own fun. I believe it is an eternal spring of enjoyment, an endlessly repeatable process with limitless variations, and will completely eliminate boredom from your life, forever.

That said, I am a pretty big fan of other people's ultramarathons, when it really comes down to it. Running around in the mountains is great, and when other people are handing you snacks every few miles, it's almost like trick-or-treating. Also, there's medical help available, restrooms, and fun things like, you know, talking to other people every once in a while instead of talking to yourself for hours on end.

I planned to carry 3.1 liters of water in my running vest, refilling at stream crossings at the 6-mile mark, 23 miles, and at 31 miles. Beyond that, I wasn't sure about water. I carried 3,420 calories in my vest:

- 2 packages of Pro Bar Bolt Chews @180 calories each
- 5 Honey Stinger Waffles (gluten-free because the gluten-free versions seem to not disintegrate as much during a long day bouncing around in a running vest) @140 calories each
- 5 packages of Clif Bloks @200 calories each
- 3 bags of Salt and Pepper Kettle Chips (smashed into little bits to pack down and for easier drinkability) @ 220 calories each
- 3 Betty Lou's Fruit Bars @ 200 calories each

I stood on top of the first summit, Stuart Peak, after almost five hours and 19 miles of running and hiking, then jogged back down to the ridge, wondering if I'd see any sort of social trail up to the summit of Mosquito Peak. There wasn't, so I kept close to the cliffs atop its east face and followed them to the top, snapped a quick, out-of-focus photo of myself on top, and then turned west for a short bushwhack along the peak's west ridge back to the trail. This, I thought, would be the biggest route-finding challenge of the day, a grand total of about three-quarters of a mile without a distinct trail.

I tromped down the trail, taking in the view from above Glacier Lake. The lake was a minimum 10-plus-mile non-motorized jaunt by any of the three routes into it, and the trail leading me down to it wasn't what you'd call buff singletrack—it's a bit adventurey to run fast on, tight, rough, with some foliage covering it for sections. It was a reminder to be careful where I put my feet. I had a Garmin InReach with me for an emergency SOS message, but a rescue/evacuation from a broken ankle would not be quick—despite the fact I had just parked my car on a city block lined with houses and started jogging a few short hours ago.

At Middle Lake at mile 24.5, I sat down on a rock to filter water through my BeFree squeeze bottle, a process that seems quick when you're just grabbing a bottle or two, but filling up a 2-liter reservoir and another half-liter bottle seemed to take hours. But with an early fall afternoon next to a mountain lake with some sun shimmering off the water, and steep cliffs dropping into the opposite shore, I had to take a minute and think: If I get one big adventure this year, and this is it, and this is the best view all day during that big adventure, that's a pretty good year.

I packed up and ran down the trail, weaving through the thick evergreen forest, and the trail widened into rough doubletrack. It was a 13-mile descent, and I enjoyed every damn step of it. I wasn't sure if I'd see another water source beyond about Mile 31, so I pulled off to top off my bottles twice when I could get to Rattlesnake Creek. And then I came to the fork in the trail. To very roughly paraphrase Helen Keller, life is either a daring adventure, or half an adventure and a slightly demoralizing but entirely reasonable hike out to a pizza and a much earlier bedtime, with a lot less inflammation.

So, I went ahead and procrastinated my pizza with a left turn, immediately realizing how much I'd underestimated how steep the climbing would be for the next five miles. A pair of trekking poles might have been nice at this point. So would a foot massage, or a helicopter ride out, I guess.

In my dream world, the sun would sit at right about the 6 p.m. level, an hour above the horizon, for the rest of my run. Or, maybe I would have brought a brighter headlamp and some backup batteries so I could confidently blast it on its brightest setting. Sadly, neither of those things were true, and from the summit of Mineral Peak near the lookout tower, I snapped photos of the final moments of the day's sunlight. It's funny, in almost every long day I've had in the mountains, I feel an urgency to hurry as the afternoon fades into evening, and the sunset draws near, and then the golden hour, and oh no if we don't get moving it's going to get dark, hurry, hurry, hurry, and then the sun goes away, and I click on my headlamp, and all of a sudden, you know, what's the rush? It's not going to get any more dark.

About five miles past the summit of Mineral Peak, the dirt road I'd been running and hiking on passed a trailhead, and I turned onto the trail. It was pretty well traveled, but with my headlamp on a fairly dim setting to preserve the battery, I remembered that I had not ever seen any of the trail for the next 12 miles—didn't know if it was hard to follow, didn't know if there were any confusing junctions, didn't know if it went through a knee-deep bog, led to a dragon's castle, whatever. I spent a lot of the next couple hours clicking my headlamp to a brighter setting, squinting into the distance, and looking down at a GPS map on my phone to make sure I was on the right trail.

One thing I know about endurance sports, at least as you're progressing into them, is that the hardest thing you've ever done becomes less hard once you've done it. And then you do the next, harder thing, and that first thing seems not nearly as bad. And then you just keep going, and going, on sort of a stair-step progression plan for idiots. A mere three and a half years ago, I ran my first 50-mile race with my friend Jayson in the woods in Wisconsin, and at mile 45 I had nothing left, mentally. We walked a lot of the last two miles of the race. I was physically capable of running at that point, but I just didn't want to. If you had offered to pay me $250 to run the last two miles, I would have declined. Maybe $1,000 would have done it. Or someone pointing a gun at my head. We did run the last few hundred yards to the finish line, and I was cooked. I couldn't believe we had finished before the cutoff. I got my finisher belt buckle, but honestly felt like it wouldn't have been undeserved if they threw me a parade, and/or erected a statue in honor of my achievement.

I thought about that for a few minutes, trudging by myself through the night in the mountains in 2020, the year of making your own fun, around Mile 47, 48, 49, 50, of a 60-mile loop I'd designed myself, thinking it would have about 12,000 feet of elevation gain, and looking down at my watch every few minutes to realize that hey, you know what, it's going to be closer to 65 miles, and 14,000 feet of elevation gain.

Then I heard something big crash in the trees to my right, off the trail. I shined my not-that-bright headlamp in that direction and saw nothing besides thick trees. OK, no big deal, probably not a bear, although my friend Aaron said he's seen a dozen bears when he's been out mountain biking in this area this summer and fall, and I've seen a bear when I was walking my dog not so far from here a month ago. I'd been running in almost complete silence for hours, in the dark, and I'd heard a couple small animals running through the brush as I approached, sometimes birds, sometimes other things, nothing more than ankle high.

But whatever the hell this was just kept crunching through tree branches, for three seconds, four seconds, six, seven seconds, Jesus, it was like someone falling off a barstool in slow motion, taking out tables and chairs as they tried to catch themselves. Whatever it was, I decided, it was probably best to not hang out long enough to introduce myself.

I hadn't realized how much my attitude had gone in the shitter for the past couple hours until I finally saw the lights of the city appear again, after hours in the dark. There was hope. I would survive. From the top of Sheep Mountain at Mile 50, which apparently has a great view during the daytime, I got enough of a cell signal to text Hilary and let her know that I would be a few, ahem, hours late.

From there, I told myself, it's pretty much all downhill. Just have to drop onto the summit of Mt. Jumbo, and then before I know it, I'll be unlocking my car door and plopping into the driver's seat and cranking the heat up for a 10-minute drive home. A coyote, I think, chattered its head off somewhere in the trees for several minutes as I got closer and closer to the saddle north of Jumbo, and finally I just said "good evening," and it stopped until I was well past.

From the saddle, it's like, what, 100 vertical feet or something to the summit? A walk in the park.

For the record, it is 800 vertical feet. I slogged uphill, pretty much ready to be done with this whole thing, especially since it had grown in distance, elevation gain, and time. Then I was on the summit, the last one of the day, and the town below seemed so quiet, like everyone had gone to bed. This is because I was standing on the summit at 1:45 a.m. on a Wednesday morning, and everyone had gone to bed.

I tried to run down the final, steeply descending two and a half miles of trail to the car, but just couldn't find the motivation, and walked big sections of it, watching my feet to make sure I didn't roll an ankle in the dark, and gradually starting to give myself a little bit of a high five. It goes. Made it. Pretty cool.

At the car, I unclipped my vest, stopped my watch, got in the car, and let out a big sigh. Then I drove to my house, where, backing the car into the driveway, I hit the fence and ripped off the front driver's side fender, which is something I would deal with tomorrow, because this day had gone on long enough.

19

SOLITAIRE

In 2020, I started trying to incorporate my iPad drawings and illustrations into some of the longer stories on my website, because it seemed like a fun idea. In reality, it was extremely labor-intensive, and some stories would take me almost two full eight-hour days of hand-writing and drawing. I don't know if people liked it better than my regular writing (do we get scared off when we see a big block of text, as opposed to some whimsically semi-unprofessional-looking all-caps handwriting?), but it seemed to draw more email feedback, so every once in a while, I would buckle down and create another story. This story was one of my favorites—kind of an ode to the things we do by ourselves, and the dreams and daydreams we have while doing them.

--

THERE WAS ONE KID STILL AT THE SKATEPARK WHEN I DROVE PAST. IT WAS A DARK MID-DECEMBER EVENING, BELOW FREEZING, BUT THE LIGHTS WERE ON, AND I GLANCED OUT THE CAR WINDOW AND SAW THE SKATER TRACING THE CONTOUR OF THE BOWL AND A PANG OF NOSTALGIA HIT ME: I KNOW THAT FEELING. OR I USED TO KNOW, ANYWAY.

IN THE PAST FEW YEARS, I'VE CONSIDERED DOZENS OF WAYS TO DEFINE "BEING YOUNG," BUT THAT SKATER REMINDED ME OF PERHAPS MY FAVORITE: STAYING OUT LATE BY YOURSELF IN THE DARK AND COLD, TRYING TO GET BETTER AT SOMETHING THAT PROBABLY SEEMS RELATIVELY MEANINGLESS TO A LOT OF PEOPLE.

"WHEN I WAS YOUNG"

- ~~WHEN I LIVED IN THAT REALLY SMALL APARTMENT~~
- ~~WHEN I HAD FEWER RESPONSIBILITIES~~
- ~~WHEN IT SEEMED LIKE MY WHOLE LIFE WAS AHEAD OF ME~~

—5 YEARS AGO

WHEN I WAS A KID, I DIDN'T HAVE A SKATEBOARD. I HAD A BASKETBALL.

FROM 5TH GRADE ON, I WAS OBSESSED WITH THE GAME.

ALL I KNEW WAS: IF I WANTED TO BE ANY GOOD, I HAD TO PRACTICE. SO I PRACTICED. I DID BALL-HANDLING DRILLS IN OUR GARAGE, WENT TO OUR LOCAL GYM WHENEVER IT WAS OPEN, AND SPENT HOURS SHOOTING JUMP SHOTS ON THE HOOP IN OUR DRIVEWAY.

IF IT RAINED, I'D PRACTICE IN THE DRIVEWAY ANYWAY. IF IT SNOWED, I'D SPEND HOURS WITH A SHOVEL AND A BROOM, MOVING SNOW AND SCRAPING ICE FROM THE CONCRETE. WE HAD ONE LIGHT THAT ILLUMINATED THE HOOP JUST ENOUGH TO PLAY AT NIGHT.

WHEN I GOT TO SEVENTH GRADE, ALL THAT PRACTICING PAID OFF: I STARTED AT POINT GUARD. I WAS SMALL, AND NOT MUCH OF A SCORING THREAT, BUT I COULD HANDLE THE BALL, AND I HUSTLED HARD.

I DIDN'T KNOW IT AT THE TIME, BUT THAT SEVENTH GRADE SEASON WOULD BE THE PINNACLE OF MY BASKETBALL CAREER. I HAD A DECENT JUMP SHOT, AND ALL THOSE HOURS OF PRACTICING MADE ME CONFIDENT WITH THE BALL IN MY HANDS, BUT...

... IN GAMES, I JUST WASN'T THAT EFFECTIVE. I DIDN'T MANAGE TO SCORE THAT MUCH, AND MADE A LOT OF MISTAKES.

(JUMPING)

(FEET STILL ON FLOOR)

Brendan Leonard, Red Oak seventh-grader, finds the going tough and has a shot attempt blocked by a Glenwood Ram in Red Oak Dec. 3. Leonard stole the ball defensively before driving to the hoop. Today, the Tigers play at Shenandoah.

But I kept playing, through eighth grade and into high school, when we moved to a town where the kids in my grade were really good at basketball. I saw less and less playing time through high school, which is what often happens when you're not that good. All that practicing hadn't translated. I had technique, but wasn't good at applying it in games. I made bad decisions on the floor, especially in front of spectators. I could never relax, focus, and just play.

BUT I KEPT PLAYING. I WAS CONVINCED I LOVED BASKETBALL. I HAD SPENT HUNDREDS OF HOURS PRACTICING AND PLAYING, HADN'T I? TO NOT KEEP TRYING WOULD MEAN ALL THAT TIME PRACTICING WAS WASTED.

A FEW WEEKS INTO MY SENIOR SEASON, I FINALLY GAVE UP. I GOT CHOKED UP WHEN I HANDED IN MY JERSEY TO MY COACH, WHO TOOK THE NEWS ABOUT AS HARD AS IF I HAD JUST TOLD HIM THE LOCKER ROOM SODA MACHINE WAS OUT OF SPRITE. IT WAS OVER. I CONSIDERED MY BASKETBALL CAREER A FAILURE. WHEN THE TEAM PLAYED GAMES ON FRIDAY NIGHTS THAT WINTER, I WAS USUALLY AT MY DISHWASHING JOB IN THE BACK OF A RESTAURANT.

A FEW YEARS LATER, I JOKINGLY TOLD MY DAD HE SHOULD HAVE NUDGED ME AWAY FROM BASKETBALL AND TOWARD SOMETHING MORE USEFUL, LIKE BAND. (IMAGINE WHERE I'D BE NOW IF I'D SPENT ALL THOSE HOURS PRACTICING THE TRUMPET!)

I FELT THAT WAY FOR A VERY LONG TIME. AFTER HIGH SCHOOL, I STOPPED WATCHING SPORTS ALTOGETHER. I DIDN'T TOUCH A BASKETBALL FOR PROBABLY 15 YEARS, AS I FOUND OTHER INTERESTS, LIKE ROCK CLIMBING AND MOUNTAINEERING.

ONE DAY AT THE YMCA IN MY PARENTS' HOMETOWN, I PICKED UP A BALL, OUT OF CURIOSITY. IT FELT ALMOST COMPLETELY FOREIGN, LIKE ALL THOSE HOURS OF PLAYING AND PRACTICING HAD BEEN ERASED SOMEHOW.

MY FIRST SHOT MISSED THE RIM BY A GOOD FOUR FEET. I LAUGHED AND TRIED AGAIN. NOTHING BUT AIR. AFTER ABOUT 10 TRIES, I FINALLY MADE A BASKET. I GOOFED AROUND FOR A FEW MORE MINUTES, AND THAT WAS THAT.

EVERY ONCE IN A WHILE, I'D THINK ABOUT BASKETBALL AGAIN—USUALLY WHEN IMPULSE-BUYING SNEAKERS FROM THE '90s. THE HEARTBREAK HAD HEALED, NOT BECAUSE OF ANY SORT OF CLOSURE, JUST BECAUSE SO MUCH TIME HAD PASSED.

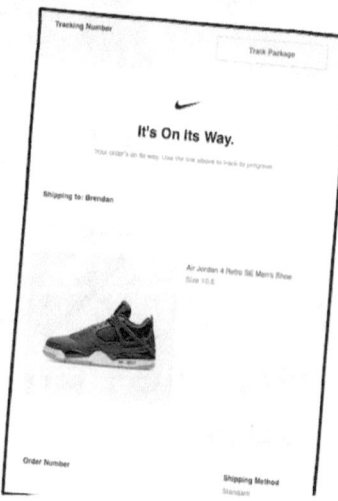

LAST OCTOBER, I TOOK OFF INTO THE MOUNTAINS AT THE EDGE OF THE TOWN WHERE I LIVE, PLANNING TO RUN AND HIKE 65 MILES BY MYSELF. IT TOOK ME 18 HOURS, AND I DIDN'T SEE ANOTHER HUMAN BEING FOR 15+ HOURS.

I DON'T LISTEN TO MUSIC OR PODCASTS WHEN I RUN, WHICH FORCES ME TO HAVE ONE THING IN MY LIFE THAT REQUIRES SILENCE. AND 18 HOURS ALONE WITH YOUR THOUGHTS IS A LONG TIME — AT LEAST BY MOST 21ST CENTURY STANDARDS.

AS I WANDERED THE TRAILS BY MYSELF THAT DAY, I STARTED THINKING ABOUT BASKETBALL, AND ALL THAT TIME I SPENT TRYING TO GET BETTER AT SOMETHING THAT ULTIMATELY DIDN'T GO ANYWHERE. AND HOW THAT DIDN'T FIT THE NARRATIVE I TELL MYSELF ABOUT WORKING HARD:

EFFORT ☒ TIME ☐ RESULTS

AND I FINALLY REALIZED:
THE PRACTICING WAS THE THING, NOT THE GAME.
THE EFFORT <u>WAS</u> THE RESULT.

I ENJOY RUNNING RACES, FROM URBAN MARATHONS WITH THOUSANDS OF PEOPLE TO MOUNTAIN ULTRAMARATHONS WITH MILES OF SOLITUDE. BUT MORE THAN RACES, I LOVE THE LONG HOURS BY MYSELF, JUST MOVING, SLIPPING ON AN EXTRA LAYER WHEN THE TEMPERATURE DROPS, CLICKING ON A HEADLAMP WHEN IT GETS DARK. THE JOY, FOR ME, IS THE LEARNED ABILITY TO JUST KEEP GOING.

JUST LIKE IN BASKETBALL, I HAVE NEVER "WON" ANYTHING DURING MY RUNNING CAREER. THERE HAS BEEN ZERO REAL SUCCESS, AS WE TRADITIONALLY DEFINE IT IN SPORTS. BUT UNLIKE BASKETBALL, NOTHING STOPS ME FROM CONTINUING TO JUST KEEP DOING IT BECAUSE I LIKE PRACTICING.

A THEME HAS COME UP IN MY READING THE PAST FEW MONTHS: THE IDEA OF HAVING SOMETHING TO BE PASSIONATE ABOUT, EVEN AS A KID, EVEN IF IT NEVER "WENT ANYWHERE."

> "I was saying to him, 'I want my daughter to do martial arts and learn to play piano.' And [Anthony Bourdain] said, 'I don't care what she does, as long as she loves it.'" I thought that was beautiful, because that is the right attitude for parenting. Not to push—to help someone be who they already are and to help someone search hard enough to find who they could be."
> —Josh Homme, The Last Curious Man, GQ, December 4, 2018

> "As our children grew up, I began to see the difference between kids who cared deeply about something—soccer, books, flute, theater, social justice, whatever—and those who didn't. You could see that even as kids, in an embryonic way, they had found some kind of meaning in their lives—and what a gift that is."
> —Bruce Handy, The Peanuts Papers

MAYBE IT'S NOT THE END RESULTS OF OUR EFFORTS, BUT THAT GIFT OF FINDING SOMETHING—OR SOME THINGS—TO CARE ABOUT, AND THROW OURSELVES INTO.

I DON'T KNOW IF ANYONE HAS FIGURED OUT WHAT WE'RE REALLY SUPPOSED TO BE DOING HERE, BUT THAT KID IN THE SKATEPARK, FLYING AROUND EVEN THOUGH EVERYONE ELSE HAS GONE HOME BECAUSE IT'S DARK AND COLD—THAT KID MIGHT BE ONTO SOMETHING.

20

POST-WORKOUT RECOVERY METHODS THAT HAVEN'T BEEN PROVEN TO WORK ... YET

I'm terrible about stretching, at all, before running, after running, whatever. I also, 99 times out of 100, would rather eat chips than drink a recovery drink. One day, while doing my usual post-workout routine, I thought, "I wonder if other people act like this too?"

--

You've just clicked the "Stop" button on your

watch, or done your last burpee, or put away your bike. You're catching your breath, a little sweaty or a lot sweaty, finished with that workout for the day. What do you do now? If you're a successful athlete, or an exercise person with a big following on social media, I'm sure you've got a high-performance recovery routine dialed. If not, you have some options beyond that perfectly formulated post-workout beverage.

Not Stretching Or Foam Rolling Or Self-Massaging/Torturing With Some Contraption
Ah yes, now that you're done, you should probably do some of those exercises or movements or stretches recommended by your physical therapist to prevent future injuries like that one you had last year, or just for general well-being or to be more prepared for the next physical thing you're going to do, but … maybe later.

Immediately Sitting Down And Looking At Your Phone For 10-45 Minutes
Better make sure your run/ride/inline skate session data uploaded to Strava, and while you have your phone out, might as well cycle through e-mail/texts/Instagram/TikTok/the news/the weather forecast/that other app you always click on because it's blue but you meant to click on the other blue app/oh shit, look at the time, what happened, better get in the shower.

Replying To Emails While Standing Next To The Shower
Just gotta get this one more email out real quick, which will definitely not lead to other emails being produced in response for you to answer later, yes, this one is the urgent one to respond to as you stand here about to step

into the shower, or maybe standing in the shower, typing with your thumb.

Eating Half A Bag Of Chips In 4 Minutes
What was that recovery drink recipe again? Maybe you'll just grab a handful of chips while you're looking for the ingredients and getting out the blender, oh yeah, chips, mmm mmm chips, chips are so good, chips chips chips, recovery chips, oh wow, you just ate half the bag. Er, maybe half—some of that was air. It always looks full in the store and then you open it and it's like whoa, optical illusion, anyway, pretty sure you didn't eat half the bag in like four minutes.

Eating A Whole Bag Of Chips in 9 Minutes
Fuck it, you deserve this, a whole bag of chips never killed anyone, you just burned 300-800 calories, and how many calories are in this bag of chips, really? Oh. Oh, that's quite a lot. Ahem, fuck it.

Lying On The Floor With Your Dog
Who's a good boy/girl, OK, just a few pets, lowers your blood pressure, good for the dog, too, OK, legs a little tired, gonna squat down here, maybe just take a knee, OK, belly rub, OK, maybe you'll just get down on the floor here for a second, oh wow, this isn't so bad.

Taking Out The Trash
You've accomplished a lot today, including that great workout, and to cap it off, you're going to grab that bag of trash and take it outside before you even take off your exercise-specific shoes. You deserve some kind of award for all this productivity, what with the workout, and the completion of a very minor but often procrastinated household task, but for now, you'll have

to make do with the feeling of personal satisfaction and accomplishment. Also, now you don't have to smoosh the trash down anymore when you're trying to fit *one more thing* in there and buy yourself a few more hours.

Recovery Drink, But By "Drink," I Mean "Leftover Pizza Eaten Over The Kitchen Sink"
Sure, you could assemble the four to 15 ingredients and put them in the blender, blend it, drink the drink, and then have to wash the blender, and there would be all sorts of great things in your body like anti-inflammatory things and protein and carbohydrates and antioxidants and all that, but when you open the fridge, oh wow, pizza! Forgot about that. Maybe not the ideal recovery meal, but at least there's a piece of a vegetable on that slice, so that counts for something, oh fuck yeah, pizza.

Recovery Drink, But By "Drink," I Mean "Beer"
There was an ad for beer that you saw somewhere, with a photo of a person on a spin bike or something like that, doing something strenuous. Maybe it's not the same brand of beer you have in the fridge but it was definitely beer, so it's probably OK to replace fluids with beer, right?

Bizarre Cramp In Bed Later
You're just about to fall asleep, or have been asleep for several hours and are rolling over and suddenly HOLY FUCK WHAT IS THAT—something seizes up and you are wildly writhing and contorting in bed, maybe trying to control it a little bit and remain silent so as not to wake up your partner, to try to alleviate the strange pain coming from your ... what the shit, is there even a

muscle there? What is going on, you didn't even use that muscle today, did you? So strange you would have a cramp after you did everything right during and after your workout, as far as recovery goes. I mean, it doesn't say it on the bag, but there have to be "electrolytes" in that bag of chips, right? Super weird.

21

26 USEFUL FACTS ABOUT RUNNING

Some of these are actual facts, and some are less, I don't know, fact-y, but maybe more like "based on a true story"? The original list was titled "26.2 Useful Facts About Running," and the last fact, the one that was .2, was just the first few words of a sentence. My editor, Hilary (who is also my wife), said that was dumb*, so I took it out.

*her actual words were probably something like "Boy, I think that might confuse people"

--

1. It is OK to take breaks while running. Sometimes breaks last a few seconds, and sometimes they last a few years.

2. There are no rules of what constitutes running, or minimum required speed, but in the sport of racewalking, one foot is required to be in contact with the ground at all times or the walker is considered to be "running."

3. There is no requirement that you have to own a couch to do the Couch to 5K program.

4. One hundred percent of the participants in the first marathon died upon completing the event.

5. No matter who you are, there is a very good chance that you can run 5 kilometers faster than you can run 5 miles. You might think, "Hell, I'll just run kilometers from now on, then," but unfortunately, that's not how it works.

6. Eliud Kipchoge, who holds the world record for the fastest marathon ever, puts his shoes on one at a time, just like you. Which is nice to think about, but he would also fucking crush you in a marathon.

7. There is no "required clothing" for running. You can wear super-short shorts, or take your shirt off in the middle of your run if you want to. The most important thing is that you're comfortable.

8. Correction: Many states and municipalities have laws requiring you to wear a certain amount of clothing in public spaces.

9. You can run in super-cushioned shoes, you can run in very minimalist shoes, and you can run barefoot. Any of these things can change your life.

10. People close to you, or people you've just met, may eventually tire of hearing how your particular footwear changed your life.

11. The top recorded running speed of a human, sprinter Usain Bolt, is 27 miles per hour. The top speed of a running grizzly bear is 35 miles per hour. Data

does not yet exist, however, on how fast a human can run while running from a bear.

12. There are no hard-and-fast rules on what you should eat and what not to eat before running; there is only your answer to the question "have you ever pooped your pants during a run?"

13. If you've been running regularly but would like to find someone to tell you you're doing it wrong, you can find them on the internet.

14. 13.1 miles is half the distance of a marathon, which is 26.2 miles. When running a marathon, at the 13.1-mile mark, you are halfway. However, at 14 miles, you are also halfway. And at 15 miles, 16 miles, 17 miles, and 18 miles, you are also still only halfway. This continues every mile until mile 25.5, when you are almost finished.

15. It is a commonly-held belief that ultrarunning is "not really running." This is only one interpretation of ultrarunning, and there is some truth in it, as running is only one component of ultrarunning. Other components of ultrarunning include but are not limited to eating snacks, hiking, running with trekking poles, hallucinating, being sad, losing toenails, bleeding, despair, blisters, talking nonsensically, shuffling, and socializing with nice people who live in the forest next to folding tables displaying snack foods.

16. People who hate running and would prefer to avoid it at all costs may refer to running as "cardio."

17. People who hate running and would prefer to avoid

it may refer to running as "running," and do it regularly for decades.

18. The first human usage of treadmills was in early 19th century English prisons. Since then, treadmills have evolved to make it possible for humans to safely watch cable news while running.

19. Lots of longtime runners say they love the simplicity of running because all you need to do it is a pair of shoes.

20. Any real runner knows that in addition to a pair of shoes, you also need a steely resolve and the hard-won psychological tools to continually, day in and day out, drag your procrastinating ass out the door and actually begin running.

21. It is generally acceptable for runners to share usage of the same running path or trail at the same time, giving space to each other when passing.

22. It is generally unacceptable for runners to share usage of the same treadmill at the same time.

23. Many musicians have written songs that mention running in a metaphorical and/or literal sense, such as Iron Maiden's "Run to the Hills," N.W.A.'s "100 Miles and Runnin," Bruce Springsteen's "Born to Run," and more cryptically, the Nirvana song "I Hate Myself and Want to Die," which is about ultramarathon running.
24. There are many ways to use technology to improve your running practice, like using an app like Strava, which, with a few clicks, will communicate with satellites in order to tabulate your time and distance

covered, or another app like GrubHub, which, with a few clicks, will enable you to have a bag of takeout food appear at your front door at the exact minute you arrive home from your run.

25. Many runners experience what's called "runner's high," a euphoric feeling caused by chemicals released by the body during or after strenuous exercise.

26. Many runners also periodically experience a completely unrelated runner's high, which is caused by extreme gastrointestinal distress while running, and then making it to a restroom *just in time* to release other chemicals produced by the body.

22

GOING FAST, GOING FAR

Something I didn't say in this essay, which is maybe relevant: I missed getting into the state spelling bee in sixth grade by getting third place instead of second place at the district spelling bee. I can no longer remember the word I spelled wrong, but the kid who beat me was named James Roach. I think he was from Greenfield, Iowa. I remember being disappointed, but maybe Future Me could have told 1990 Me, "Hey man, it's OK. This will fit really well into your life narrative in 30 years."

--

Even when I was just taping off my steps before the race started, I was comparing myself to the other runners. I don't remember many of the moments of the actual 100 meters in high school, but I remember walking off steps around the curve in my lane on the track, and that the distance between my two pieces of athletic tape was much longer than anyone in the other seven lanes in the 4 x 100 relay. As our third runner, I eventually got up to speed, but I needed a long runway. The second leg runners would come flying in, and everyone in the other lanes would need six, eight, maybe 10 steps to get up to speed for an efficient baton handoff. I would count off more like 20 or 22 steps.

I was the direct opposite of my friend Chris, who led off our relay, and was capital-e Explosive out of the blocks. In his football cleats, I would have no doubts about betting on him vs. a brick wall standing five feet away from him. At 160 pounds, he was the lightest shot-putter to qualify for the state track meet that year. Chris would start off our 4 x 100 relay, hand off to Casey, who would later be a college athlete. Casey would catch me just as I (finally) got up to speed, hand the baton to me, and I'd hammer as fast as I could for 100 meters until I passed to Ryan, who would also go on to be a college wide receiver. Ryan would fly to the finish line, sometimes passing a few people on his way.

I had little real athletic success in high school, but near the tail end of my junior year, I started to develop some speed. Our track team wasn't exactly the flagship athletic program of our small school—we had a cinder track and rarely hosted a home track meet—but it was my biggest success, mostly on our 4 x 100 and 4 x 200 relay teams. I had high hopes we'd actually make the state track meet in something and I'd get to go, and the 4 x 100 was our best chance.

For a couple months that year, as part of those relay teams, I felt fast. We did well at most of our meets, and as the season went on, we were in reach of a qualifying time for State Track. In the end, though, we came up four-hundredths of a second short. It was late in the school year, we were graduating, and "barely not making it" had started to feel like a bit of a theme in my life.

I had just missed graduating Magna Cum Laude by three-thousandths of a grade point, something that could have been rectified by not fucking around in gym class for four years (or maybe fucking around just a tiny bit less during just one of eight semesters), and I hadn't gotten into any great colleges. At age 18, when you might love to see a sign from the universe indicating some sort of direction for the rest of your life, I began to realize "directly competing with other people" was probably not, for me, going to be a path to success or fulfillment.

There are plenty of ways to be "the best" when you're in high school—conference champs, all-district, valedictorian, homecoming/prom royalty, most likely to succeed, but most of us graduate with lots of experience being "not the best" at a lot of things. There's only one Number One, obviously, and then the rest of us. After my final track meet, I had no immediate reason to keep running 100-meter dashes and 200-meter dashes, or running at all, for that matter.

I didn't get back into regular running until 18 years later, minus a short break in 2006 when I trained for and ran a road marathon "to see what it was like" and also to make myself quit smoking. It worked: I found out what it was like, didn't enjoy it all that much, and quit smoking.

Plenty of adults, such as myself, get turned off by running because we think we should be fast, and we suck at being fast. It's pretty easy to think that way, especially if you wear a watch, or track your mileage and time with a smartphone app, or run an organized race. The numbers are right there: You ran that mile in 9:38. You got 13,942nd place overall in the race. Of the human beings of your gender within 5 years of your age who signed up for a specific race in your region, you were the 182nd best at covering 6.2 miles efficiently on foot.

In the middle of my 18-year break from running, though, I picked up this magical book called *Born to Run*, had my mind blown, and found a different reason to run: To answer the question "How far can I go?" Which was far more interesting to me than "How do I compare with other people covering a certain distance on a certain day in a certain place?"

I trained for, entered, and completed ultramarathon-distance trail races—50 km, 50 miles, 100 km, 100 miles—and of course, was timed and ranked according to how fast I went. But the point, to me, was answering the question, "Can I do it?" And it was great to have someone take care of planning the route and supplying the snacks and water for me so I could just concentrate on going forward. For me, right now, that's where the real magic lies: the ability to just keep moving. On the trail. With a bunch of other people who aren't so much competition, more like fellow idiots.

How fast we go, of course, can be a good metric for our progress: What's the absolute shortest amount of time we can cover a certain distance, or how does one mile at X:00 pace feel, or can we shave a couple seconds off last week's time running up a certain hill or segment. But going farther is, at this point in my life, more exciting. I can look at a map and figure out a new route, maybe to a new place or on a new trail, knowing that with a certain amount of calories and water stashed in my vest, I can comfortably cover X distance—or, let's be honest, semi-comfortably or uncomfortably.

I co-host a running podcast a couple times a month, and one of the questions I always like to ask our interviewees is: How are you getting better at running without necessarily getting faster? Because all of us eventually reach an age when we're not getting faster. And when we get to that age, and finally have to admit that, it can be hard and even heartbreaking if we don't have other reasons to keep going. Of course, nowadays, I'm more than comfortable admitting my fastest 100-meter and 200-meter efforts are behind me—but my best running days, I believe, are not.

I took three weeks off of running this winter because of a sinus infection, and whatever fitness and endurance I had pretty much evaporated. I started running again, easy at first, and then met up with a friend after about a week and a half of regular runs. We ran a mile, hiked up a steep climb for a few minutes, ran the trail down, and then separated again for my final mile home. Somewhere in that last mile, for about a block, I realized I was a little tired, but I felt OK—OK enough to just keep going if I wanted to. Which is a pretty good reason to keep doing it.

23

"PARKING LOT LAPS": A RATIONALE

Maybe it's just me, but I think one of the reasons we do creative things like writing, photography, filmmaking, and other pursuits, is that we believe we have something unique to say. I don't want to go as far as to say that we do it because we think we're "special," but there might be some truth to that too, as egotistical as it sounds. The funny thing about that is, especially in regards to this piece, is that art is really successful when it captures a feeling that a lot of other people can relate to. So if you think you're weird or unique, isn't making creative work just sort of a way of putting out a signal to find some other people who are weird/unique, in the same way you are?

This one is about this weird thing I do with running stats, and I thought a handful of other runners might also do the same thing. It apparently resonated with a few people, and ended up getting mentioned in a New York Times *piece, so obviously the weird thing I do isn't that weird, or unique.*

--

"PARKING LOT LAPS": A RATIONALE

I TRY TO NOT SAY "THERE ARE TWO TYPES OF PEOPLE IN THE WORLD..."

BUT IF I TOLD YOU THAT AT THE END OF MY RUNS, I LOOK AT MY WATCH AND IF IT SAYS I'VE RUN 5.89 MILES, I WILL RUN PAST MY HOUSE FOR A WHILE AND THEN BACK IN ORDER TO GET MY WATCH TO CLICK OVER TO 6.00 MILES, I'M PRETTY SURE YOU'D HAVE ONE OF TWO REPLIES:

○ a. "That's the dumbest
     fucking thing ever"

○ b. "oh, I do that too"

I GET IT. ACTUALLY, I WOULD ADD A THIRD OPTION TO THAT:

> ○ a. "That's the dumbest fucking thing ever"
>
> ○ b. "oh, I do that too"
>
> ○ c. (both of the above)

If you are a runner who also does this sort of thing, you probably have your own reasons.

If you don't, you might think, "Why would someone do that? Who cares if you run 5.89 miles instead of 6.00 miles? Your body doesn't know the difference."

(Also, I might as well admit that I actually go 6.03 miles, because early on in my use of Strava, the upload between my watch and the app somehow cut off .01 mile a few times, so I go an extra .03 mile now)

PEOPLE HAVE ALL SORTS OF DIVERSE GOALS FOR THEIR RUNNING. SOME COMMON GOALS INCLUDE QUALIFYING FOR THE BOSTON MARATHON OR THE WESTERN STATES ENDURANCE RUN, RUNNING A SUB-4-HOUR MARATHON, OR TO SOMEDAY HAVE EIGHT TOENAILS INSTEAD OF TEN.

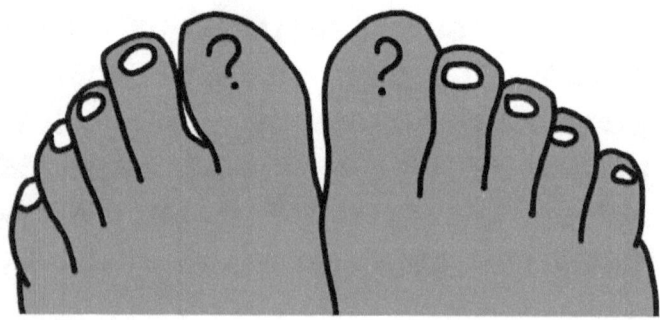

I ONLY HAVE ONE GOAL MOST OF THE TIME, AND IT'S A CERTAIN NUMBER OF MILES PER WEEK. THE NUMBER USUALLY FLUCTUATES BY YEAR AND BY SEASON, BUT IS MOSTLY BASED AROUND AN AMOUNT OF PIZZA, BREAKFAST BURRITOS, AND ICE CREAM I'D LIKE TO EAT WITHOUT GAINING TOO MUCH WEIGHT. THIS WEEK, FOR EXAMPLE, IT'S 25 MILES.

AT THE TOP OF THE CLIFF, I AM MEETING GOALS AND DEADLINES, AT A HEALTHY AND FULFILLING LEVEL OF PRODUCTIVITY. BUT I AM ONE SMALL METAPHORICAL GUST OF WIND AWAY FROM GOING OFF THE CLIFF.

(THE BEST VERSION OF ME)

(THE VERSION OF ME IN WHICH ALL MY NEGATIVE TENDENCIES BASICALLY BECOME MY ENTIRE PERSONALITY)

THE BOTTOM OF THE CLIFF IS WHERE THE MOST FALLIBLE VERSION OF ME LIVES. ON THE TOP OF THE CLIFF IS THE VERSION OF ME THAT TRIES TO IDIOT-PROOF MY LIFE WITH SAFEGUARDS TO PREVENT THE FALLIBLE ME FROM TAKING OVER.

ME	ALSO ME
PRONE TO OVERSLEEPING	SETS TWO ALARMS ON WATCH PLUS TWO ALARMS ON PHONE (W/ THAT AIR RAID SIREN RINGTONE)

ME	ALSO ME
PRONE TO FORGETTING WHERE I PARKED AT THE AIRPORT/ MY HOTEL ROOM NUMBER	TAKES PHONE PHOTOS JUST IN CASE

TO A LOT OF PEOPLE, 5.89 MILES IS JUST AS GOOD AS 6.00 MILES. A LOT OF PEOPLE ARE CAPABLE OF DRINKING ONE BEER AND STOPPING, AND/OR EATING A SINGLE SERVING OF OREOS (WHICH IS "3 COOKIES" ?!?!). I APPLAUD THOSE PEOPLE.

I HAVE, OVER MANY YEARS, COME TO THE REALIZATION THAT I AM NOT ONE OF THOSE PEOPLE. IF 5.89 MILES EQUALS 6.00 MILES TODAY, AT THE END OF THE WEEK, 21 MILES WILL EQUAL 25, AND PRETTY SOON, I'LL BE AT

11 MILES A WEEK,

AND THEN

7 MILES A WEEK,

AND

THEN

That's why I have to run the last .11 miles, or .14, or .37, or whatever, even if it's around the parking lot at the trailhead, or around my block while my neighbors look at me and scratch their heads.

Or at least that's what I tell myself.

I'm fully aware that it's ridiculous, but so is running when no one's chasing you, when you think about it. So is lifting heavy things and setting them down the same place you picked them up, and riding a bicycle that goes nowhere.

It's all ridiculous, and we're all ridiculous. It's just a personal preference of what we're doing ridiculously.

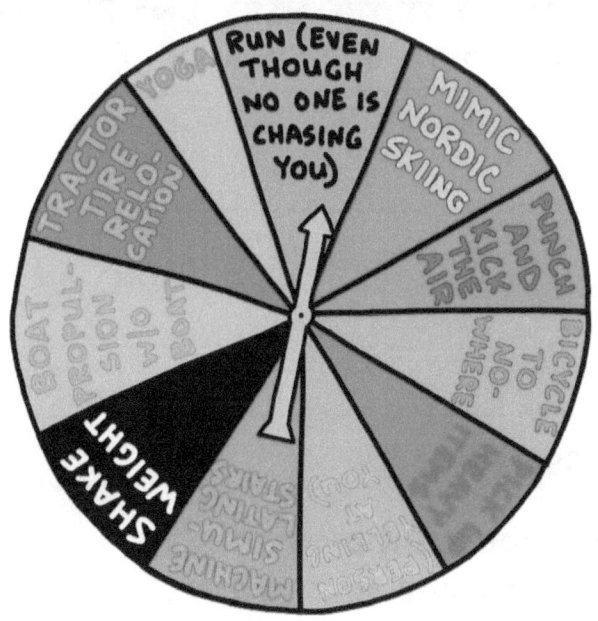

BUT IF YOU'RE ONE OF THOSE PEOPLE WHOSE STRAVA MAPS LOOK LIKE A TORNADO AT THE VERY END BECAUSE YOU HAD TO GET TO X.00 (OR X.03),

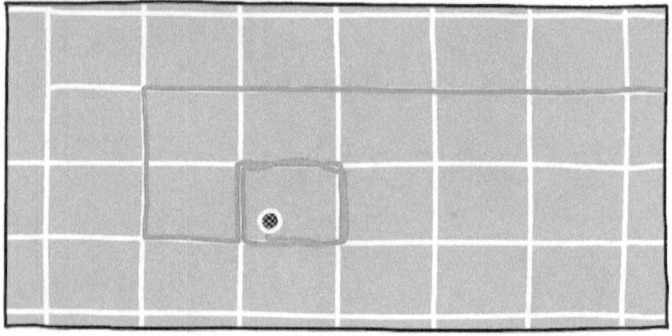

I SEE YOU.

AND YOU'RE RIDICULOUS.
BUT YOU ARE NOT ALONE.

24

RACE REPORT: THE RUT 50K

When I started studying journalism at the University of Montana 150 years ago, my dream was to get to write about music. But by the time I graduated, it became clear that it would be easier, and probably more appropriate, to try to make a living writing about outdoor adventure. I was spending my weekends going hiking and climbing mountains, not going to shows. My first magazine article appeared in IDAHO Magazine *and I got paid $40. It was not huge, but it was a start, and the model was: Go do fun stuff, pay attention to your experience, come back, and try to write something compelling about it. It's a simple formula, and I don't do as much of it as I used to, but as I was doing The Rut 50K in Montana, I started to get a pretty good feeling that I had enough material to make something fun out of it when I got home.*

--

High on the east ridge of Lone Peak, at about 10,500 feet or so, The Rut 50K started to feel like a cartoon, in which an idiot, me, runs and hikes up an incline at a fast (for me) but hopefully sustainable pace, as the grade gradually gets steeper and steeper, until, just before the summit, the idiot tips over backwards and rolls back to the start.

This, of course, is not true. The elevation map of the race course actually looks like this:

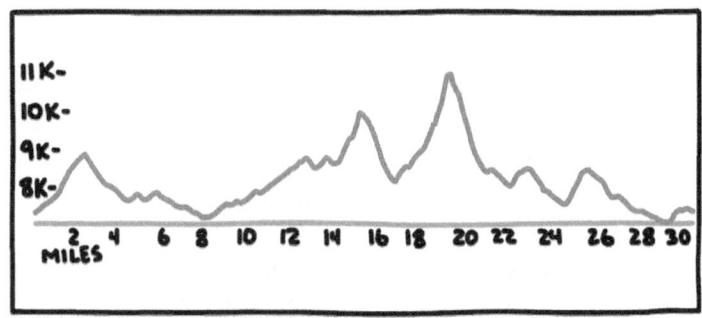

But right around Mile 20, I felt like I'd been carefully picking my way up Lone Peak's east ridge for six hours, three feet in front of a guy from Eugene the entire time. With the steep terrain, fatigue, altitude, a decreased amount of readily available oxygen for breathing, and the mental exhaustion of climbing a never-ending pile of rocks while trying to not dislodge anything onto people below me, many elements were coming together to crush my morale, and me.

This is also not true. I was just one of 500 or so people to sign up for The Rut 50K this year. The Rut is an annual event that is essentially a European-style sky race held in Big Sky, Montana, designed by two American sadomasochists named Mike (Foote and Wolfe), with several events ranging from a Vertical Kilometer to the 50K. One way to look at the 50K race might be, "Hey, I ran the Chicago Marathon last year, and The Rut 50K is only five miles longer than that."

Here are some words and phrases from the website for The Rut 50K:

- "extremely challenging"

- "EXTREMELY STEEP & TECHNICAL"
- "exposure"
- "potential rockfall hazard"
- "true mountain course"
- "rockfall hazards"
- "mountainous and technical nature"

It's probably good policy for mountain running race organizers to use strong language in describing their events, just so no one gets in over their head and then later says things like "no one told me would be this hard," or "suddenly, there I was, staring death in the face," or "[sounds of a person sitting on a pile of rocks and weeping uncontrollably]." But also, you could probably be forgiven for a tiny bit of skepticism as far as race marketing is concerned, i.e. "I don't know, has anyone ACTUALLY died doing this 'Death Race' we're signing up for?"

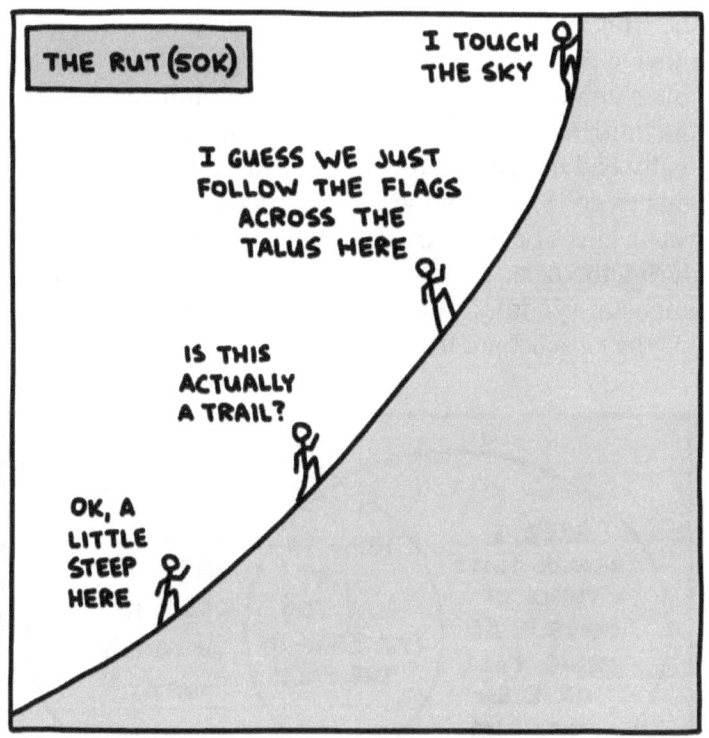

There is at least one spot on The Rut 50K where you could legitimately fall, and possibly not stop falling until you were dead and/or have way more than 208 bones in your body.

I did not, as may be obvious at this point, die doing The Rut. I did perhaps underestimate it a tiny bit.

The race started at 6:00 a.m., a few minutes before sunrise, in three waves, five minutes apart, each wave a few hundred runners jogging uphill, a stream of headlamps, nerves, and chatter leaving the Big Sky Resort base area. Where should I start? Certainly not at the front of the first wave, where the elite runners and other super-mutants would be, ripping off three-minute miles uphill or whatever. Probably not at the back of the third wave, based on my previous race results. I really had no idea what to expect, so I did what I always do: Start way too far back in the pack, and then waste tons of energy frantically trying to pass people during the race. This is probably some combination of impostor syndrome and Midwestern over-politeness, or maybe I'm just not that smart.

Another role I had signed up for: running with a younger friend, Devon, and theoretically helping him not go too fast for the first few miles of the race. Devon had finished an 18-day traverse of the Wind River Range literally 60 hours before the start, and is a full decade-plus younger than me, so for the first nine miles, we settled somewhere in between me holding him back and him dragging me up the trail. When the route went from fire road to singletrack, there were bottlenecks of single-file lines of people, where we literally stood waiting in line for a couple minutes.

In the first nine miles, in any spot where the trail widened in the forest, Devon and I accelerated around runners in front of us, sometimes one at a time, sometimes a handful of people. I did have a small bit of anxiety knowing that at a certain point, the course would hit a 1.2-mile section climbing 2,000 feet up the ridge of Lone Peak, where it would be pretty difficult to pass anyone without them very graciously stepping off to the side of the path, so I was motivated to pass people early on, where it was easy and safe. But I had more anxiety about running myself into the ground in the first 10 miles of the race by going way too fast way too early. Just before Mile 9, I told Devon to go ahead without me, because although I am not smart, I am also not proud, and he shot off like a gazelle through the trees, finally free.

I had thoroughly studied the course map and elevation profile in the days and weeks leading up to the race, but still found myself surprised at all the ups and downs as we tromped through the forest, popped out above treeline, then dropped back into the trees again. I had downloaded the GPX map of the course onto my phone and could open it at any time to see where I was on the course, but I decided to just keep plodding on in ignorance, following the flags. Somewhere around Mile 14 or so, the course went from what I would call "pretty normal" to "OK, this is not an actual hiking trail that anyone uses for anything not named 'The Rut.'" At that point, I was thankful I had talked myself into carrying trekking poles, ignoring the advice of at least one friend, who was well-meaning, but who also drastically overestimated my VO2 max. I mean, they weigh 10.5 ounces, and are very handy when you want to lean on something and shed a few tears, instead of collapsing all the way to the ground to convulse with sobs.

I managed to under-eat the morning of the race, and was hungry the entire day, shoving down Clif Bloks and Honey Stinger Waffles whenever I could, often chewing while mouth-breathing in huge gasps as I hiked steep uphills. I had packed something like 2,000 calories for the day in my vest, in hopes that it would keep me from wasting time at aid stations, because I often unintentionally spend more time gazing at the layout of M&Ms, chips, pickles, Oreos, etc. than most people do putting together a plate at the Sizzler salad bar, and then end up confused at how six people passed me in the time I took to fill one water bottle and walk away with a double-handful of Cheez-Its.

At the 14.5-mile mark, we started climbing up steep talus. The pack had thinned out and I had found a pretty appropriate spot, every once in a while passing someone or letting someone pass me, but for the most part able to settle in, put my head down, and watch my feet. Surely, I thought—without actually checking my GPS app to see where we were on the course—this must be the big climb up Lone Peak. Here we go.

Imagine my internal dismay 40 minutes later when the route started going downhill from a high point of about 10,100 feet. Going down always feels good, but not as good when you know you'll have to climb right back up every single foot you descend. We dropped to 8,280 feet, hitting a fire road, which was nice for a few minutes, I guess. But the course's high point was

11,166 feet, somewhere above us.

If you hit Mile 17 during a flat-ish 50K, you're psyched! You're more than halfway to the finish! If you hit Mile 17 during The Rut, you are ... not as psyched! You are more than halfway to the finish ... in mileage only! You are about to spend an hour or an hour and a half grinding up a steep incline, 2,900 feet in 2.5 miles! You will "run" a 40-minute mile! Your fancy GPS watch will, instead of showing your pace per mile, will display a series of dashes, basically saying "you are not moving—are you OK?"

The good thing is, you eventually get to the top. Maybe you're motivated by finishing the race, maybe because everywhere you look you're surrounded by angular blocks of rock that would not be comfortable to sit or lie down on, maybe because finishing the race will be a visceral metaphor for other things you hope to face in life, or maybe because you know deep down that literally hundreds of other people have done the same thing so you can too, and some of those people have literally gotten a complimentary Run the Rut tattoo at the finish line, a real tattoo, not a temporary one, because that is a thing they do at this race.

At the top of Lone Peak are some nice people handing out water and snacks, including, when I was there, a shirtless man wearing a full-length fur coat. The actual aid station we passed through was a solid 30 or 40 vertical feet below the summit of Lone Peak itself, and for a moment, my inner peak-bagger felt conflicted about getting this close to the summit after working that hard to get there and not actually tagging it, but I decided to keep moving forward, and down the mountain.

The route down Lone Peak is steep, starting with dinner-plate talus, then scree, then steep trails. I had seen people wearing running gaiters at the beginning of the race, and as I made my way down and kicked rocks into my own shoes, I thought this might be the one place I could have used them in my life. Alas, I did not have any. Nor did I take the time to do proper self-care/self-preservation practices, like, I don't know, emptying the rocks out of my shoes at any point during the final 11 miles of the race.

I enjoy lying to myself during races, a tactic I believe is a form of positive self-talk. I do not enjoy it when I catch myself in the lies I have told myself earlier. Such as "You'll start feeling better when you only have five miles to go," or "That weird feeling in your lower intestine is unlikely to turn into anything remotely explosive before the end of the race," or in this case, "That was the last big climb—it should be a cruise from here," and "We're back below treeline, so it's probably just gently rolling from here on out."

I had read some race reports from previous years, so I should have been well aware that the last 10 miles or so seemed to be generally demoralizing. True, all the "big" climbs were out of the way, and most of what was left was below treeline. But before the finish, we still had a 500-foot climb, a 900-foot climb, and a 400-foot climb. I started up the beginning of the 900-foot climb, on a steep trail that I'm pretty sure I heard had a rope on it at one point for runners to use to pull themselves up the incline, and found myself surrounded by a glut of people in various states of mild to extreme discontent:

our pace slowed to an uphill crawl, some people muttering half-jokes about how terrible they felt, others hunched over with their hands on their knees or leaning on a tree, maybe about to throw up. I kept going, thankful I had trekking poles, both as life support and security blanket.

This, I think, is where many people start to hate the Rut. You start to ask yourself what the point of going up and down these hills is (as if the whole idea of the race isn't also contrived and pointless, in the grand scheme of human existence), why they would send you this way instead of a route that's more friendly (or even just flat), and maybe why you didn't sign up for the 28K or the 11K instead of the 50K.

The singletrack gave way to a road, which started to ease up as I inched closer to an aid station. Spectators waiting for the runner(s) they knew to come through dotted the sides of the road, cheering everyone who came past. One woman yelled, "Nice job, you're almost there," and I said "Thank you, existentially, we're already there, aren't we?" I power-hiked into the aid station and a young gentleman named Dash filled my water bottles and I grabbed a couple half-bananas and gulped them down.

The course wound mostly downhill through intermittent forest, finally topping out on the last climb a half-mile from the finish line, where a couple guys sitting on the side of the fire road told me Nice job, you're really, really done with the last climb now, and then another guy 100 feet later said "Those guys are lying," and I laughed as I jogged past, the ski area base within view, and around the corner from that, the finish line. Which is where, I think, people begin the transition from hating the Rut to loving the Rut. As is common in this sport, the same person who, at 1 p.m. one day carries themselves along a trail on fumes of motivation and curses everything that brought them to that point, 24 or 48 hours later will earnestly tell people who ask about their race, "It was great." Whatever that means.

25

MY FRIEND SAYS IT'S THE GREATEST RACE IN THE WORLD

Because of circumstances described in this piece, I ended up running the 2021 New York City Marathon alone. This enabled me to do two things: Notice what was happening and how I felt, and to try to run fast (for me), which is not something I had ever tried to do prior to 2021. But for some reason, I thought I would give it a shot this year, and maybe I'd finish fast enough to vault myself into a faster starting corral in a future NYC Marathon. I don't know if it was the effort, or being in New York after a couple years away, or some weird pent-up stuff from almost two years of living through the Covid-19 pandemic, or what, but it felt like something was really happening during this race.

--

Just after the crest of the Verrazzano-Narrows Bridge, the longest and highest climb of the New York City Marathon, around Mile 1.0, one of the MTA Bridge and Tunnel employees yelled some encouragement to those of us in the final starting wave of the race as we jogged across the span almost 700 feet in the air, Manhattan taking up the horizon to the left, Brooklyn and open ocean to the right.

"Come on," a voice barked from a group of guys in safety yellow sitting on the back of a truck as I passed.

"We've been out here all morning," he continued. "It's freezing." He was right—it was a chilly morning, and there aren't many places on the bridge to get out of the cold breeze. The encouragement was starting to turn into half-support, half-joke. Here is a man after my own heart. He finished with:

"Get off the bridge."

I started laughing mid-stride and did what everyone says not to do: run fast for the entire downhill section of the bridge, into Brooklyn.

--

I had planned on a pretty mellow marathon day—no rush, just go for a nice jog, easy pace, stop and say hi to a couple friends who would be out cheering, maybe hang out for a couple minutes with them. My friend Syd and I would be doing the race together, and last time we did it in 2019, we finished in a fairly leisurely (for us) 4:50.

Then Syd strained his hamstring nine days before the race, and his 2021 race was in jeopardy. He spent the week in physical therapy appointments, but by Friday, running more than a mile was still a no-go.

So, he said, he was just going to walk the whole thing

instead. I said I wasn't sure he would have that much fun doing that, but Syd loves the NYC Marathon. He does not love running, but he was born here, and he loves the race that calls itself "the world's marathon," and is also his hometown race, which he's run a dozen times now. Every year, he begins his day by getting on the 1 train at the 66th St. station, getting off at South Ferry, taking the ferry to Staten Island, a bus to the start village below the Verrazzano-Narrows Bridge, and then running the race, crossing the finish line and then walking a few blocks back to his apartment.

Instead of running with me in the last starting wave at noon, Syd decided he'd leave with his assigned wave at 9:55 a.m. and have a two-hour head start on me. We did some rough math at a restaurant on Friday evening and figured that there was a good chance we'd finish pretty close to each other, depending on how fast he walked and how fast I ran. And also, if his hamstring held together and he made it to the finish line.

I had not prepared for the race very intelligently. I hadn't run more than eight miles or so on pavement at one time the entire year, since I'd spent most of my time training for trail races. I had just finished one of those races, a 100K, 22 days ago. The previous Friday, I did the Presidential Traverse in New Hampshire with my friend Doug, covering 21 miles and 8,300 feet of elevation gain, and during which I slipped on a wet rock and fell directly on my ass but also caught part of my fall with the ball of my left foot. Nothing was broken, but it was painful to go up and down stairs the next two days.

I spent most of the Saturday before the race walking

around Greenwich Village and drinking coffee, not wanting to spend my time sitting in an Airbnb with my feet up. A voice in my head started saying things like, "Maybe you should just try to run fast tomorrow." Sure, Voice In My Head, I could do that. But it might not be—how would you say—something a smart person would do?

--

While drinking coffee at 5 a.m. the morning of the race, I committed to non-committal: I'd "just" "kind of try" to "run a little faster" at the beginning and see how it went, and maybe I'd feel good and keep going. Maybe I'd feel like garbage and decide to settle into a slower pace. Either way, I figured best-case I'd break four hours, and worst-case I'd come in around 4:20 or 4:30. A few years ago, I ran a bunch of self-guided marathons throughout the year, and if it was reasonably flat and I was feeling good, I could usually finish a marathon in about 4:20. One time I went really hard and ran one in 3:48, all by myself, in the park, carrying 60 ounces of water. So, in theory, I could maybe do it again?

It is impossible to exaggerate the energy of the NYC Marathon spectators. There are truly very few sections, of short distances, in which you are not being watched, encouraged, cheered at, or serenaded by either a live band or a DJ. Almost all of those sections are on the five bridges you cross: the Verrazzano from Staten Island into Brooklyn, the Pulaski Bridge from Brooklyn into Queens, the Queensboro Bridge from Queens into Manhattan, the Willis Avenue Bridge from Manhattan into The Bronx, and the Madison Avenue Bridge from

The Bronx back into Manhattan. Lots of marathoners walk the uphill sections of the bridges, so the slowed group speed, plus the relative silence, plus the uphill grade, can make the bridges feel long, arduous, and morale-dampening.

The Verrazzano-Narrows Bridge drops runners into Bay Ridge, the beginning of the Brooklyn section of the race. I had run fast enough up and down the bridge that I could only see a few runners ahead of me, all of us spread out by a hundred feet or more, as we started to encounter the first of the spectators lining the streets, cheering and holding signs welcoming us to Brooklyn. With how spread out we were thanks to the 2021 marathon having only 30,000 entrants compared to 53,000 in 2019, and the starting waves staggered with more time in between, the early spectators really felt like they were cheering just for me.

I have spent much more of my race time running trail ultramarathons, which require lots of hours plodding along in solitude with few distractions from the pain in your legs and the number of miles you have left. The New York City Marathon is on the opposite end of the spectrum: You experience a sensory bombardment that might be a bit terrifying if it didn't feel so positive and uplifting the entire time.

In several sections, the roar of the crowd is loud enough and close enough that earplugs would definitely not be a ridiculous idea. Most of the time, spectators stand well back from the street, but in many places, they narrow the race course, drawn in by the gravity of the runners, their enthusiasm pushing them unconsciously forward. At one point in Williamsburg, the course tightened into a tunnel of screaming people, leaving only 15 feet or so for runners to squeeze through. Some people hold out paper towels or tissues for runners to grab as they pass, or half-bananas, or candy, and sometimes spectators have bought a case of water bottles to hand out.

I have never left my house to go cheer for people running any sort of footrace, and I don't know if I understand what motivates people to do it, but I am thankful that they do it. I don't know why they care if perfect strangers feel encouraged and/or even loved for a few hours as they struggle through the streets—all I can say is that I have never felt so supported doing anything in my entire life as I have in New York during the marathon. I imagine it's something like a basketball player feels as they step up to the foul line with the chance to put their team ahead with one second remaining on the clock, and the crowd stands up, cheers, claps, and fills the arena with noise—but when you're running the marathon, there's no possibility of letting anyone down. The ball will not bounce off the back of the rim. You just keep moving forward. Even if you staggered and passed out on the street, I have a feeling you'd be immediately carried off the course and to medical assistance within seconds by two to six New Yorkers. Actually, they might just pick you up and half-carry you down the race course until you got your feet under you again, who knows.

A few years back, I was exiting a subway station somewhere in the Bronx, plodding up a flight of stairs a few feet behind an older woman carrying a shopping bag. At each step, she would set the bag down on the next step, then move her feet up, slowly going up the stairwell, holding up everyone below her on the stairs as we waited. Suddenly, a man stepped out from behind me and walked into the flow of people coming down the stairs. He reached over and took the woman's shopping bag out of her hand without saying a word, and then quickly charged up the last eight or ten steps. At the top of the stairs, he set the shopping bag down and walked off, without even a glance back. When she reached the top of the stairs, the woman picked up her bag and carried on.

As we were waiting for the race to start that morning, I joked to Syd that I thought it would be hilarious to carry a huge map of the race course for the first couple miles, holding it out in front of you and saying things like, "we go straight here" and "we turn left up ahead somewhere." Syd laughed and said it would be IMPOSSIBLE to get lost during this race, and I think he meant literally, but maybe also spiritually, in a sort of collective New York humanism way.

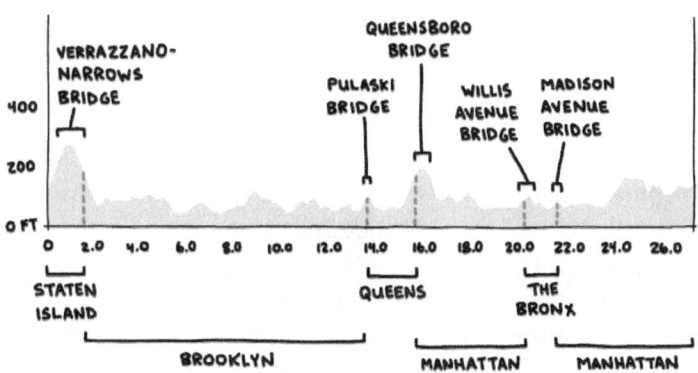

One way to look at a marathon is that you're going to

feel like shit eventually, and you're just trying to hold it off as long as possible. You hope it doesn't happen until mile 23 or 24, but if you go out too fast, you can find yourself in a bad way much sooner than you might expect. I went out too fast.

I did not research any sort of race strategy or consult any sort of expert or coach. I just thought that morning that I'd try to run a bunch of 9-minute miles early on in the race and get them "in the bank," so to speak, and the more 9-minute miles I ran, the closer I'd be to a sub-4-hour pace. Maybe I could afford to take it a little easy near the end and jog some 10-minute miles, if I didn't waste too much time stopping to refill my water bottle and/or talking to people.

I stopped to pee once, around Mile 8, picking the absolute Worst Porta-Potty on the Race Course, the inside of which had been sprayed by, well, someone having a much less gastrointestinally stable day than I was having. I bolted in and bolted out as quickly as I could, rubbing way too much hand sanitizer on my hands as I ducked the tape to head back onto the race course.

I stopped to talk to friends in Fort Greene, maybe for a minute or slightly less, and again around Mile 16 just after the Queensboro Bridge, when my friend Greg handed me a banana, effectively paying me back for the banana I'd given him when I was watching the race and he was running it in 2014. I grabbed water at several of the later water stations, and a full-size Reese's Peanut Butter Cup and a bag of M&Ms from a guy handing out leftover Halloween candy around mile 17. And then at about Mile 21, someone yelled my name from the right side of the race course: Syd. I stopped to walk with him for a few feet, checking in on how his hamstring felt, and enjoying the feeling of just not running for a while. I was very, very tempted to just chuck my whole idea of running fast and just walking the rest of the race with Syd. But he told me to keep going, so eventually I started jogging again.

By that point, with five miles left, I was starting to drag. I tried lying to myself, saying things like "I feel strong" and "I feel good" in my head as my muscles stiffened and I was sure my "running" "form" was starting to like the Tin Man from *The Wizard of Oz*. And then at Mile 23, the race course climbs the hill up 5th Avenue, because, well, fuck you. That's what the course has always done, and probably always will do as long as they have this marathon, and if it makes you sad and want to cry because you're tired, that's just the way it is, but to finish the race you still have to drag your carcass up it, one way or another. People, myself included, were struggling. I tried to pass as many people as I could, hoping the mini-sprints to get around other runners might keep my per-mile pace at a respectable speed. A woman who was at least six months pregnant, wearing a shirt reading "Baby on Board" on the back, appeared, and I paused to tell her nice job, because OK, I was really trying hard and going through an intense personal struggle here at mile 22, but not, you know, constructing a human being in my abdomen during the marathon.

We turned into the park at 86th Street, and the spectators were all there, screaming, standing mostly off to the side but sometimes almost in the way, looking for their friend or family member, and they were all clean and showered and not sweaty and wearing nice clothes and just in general the complete opposite of how I felt and looked, and I kind of wanted them to all go away so I could just do this last bit of suffering to the finish line in private. Time slowed down, and minutes started to take twice as long as they did earlier in the race, and oh fuck me, that's right, there are a couple more little hills, ugh.

And then all of a sudden we turned onto Central Park South and out of nowhere, I caught a sob in the back of my throat, something in the way the whole scene in front of me was framed and happening, and I don't know where it came from, and for a second I thought I might just start weeping in front of all these strangers as I ran the last mile but I didn't really care if I did or if they cared or noticed, and two breaths later it just disappeared. My legs fucking hurt and I kept trying to tell myself to lift my knees but it felt like I was running in sand.

But I wasn't; I was still making progress, and I looked at my watch and I had plenty of time, and unless I somehow tripped and fell and knocked myself unconscious in the next 14 minutes, I would finish in under four hours. Which is a totally arbitrary measurement of velocity over a semi-arbitrary distance some guy in ancient Greece allegedly ran once, and then we somehow decided that hundreds of cities around the world should create mass running events of that same distance, including New York. And all of that would be a lot to explain if an alien landed here and ran up next to me on Central Park South and asked what I was doing, and that's a weird thing to be thinking about, but so is almost bursting into tears after running for three hours and 50 minutes straight for no real reason.

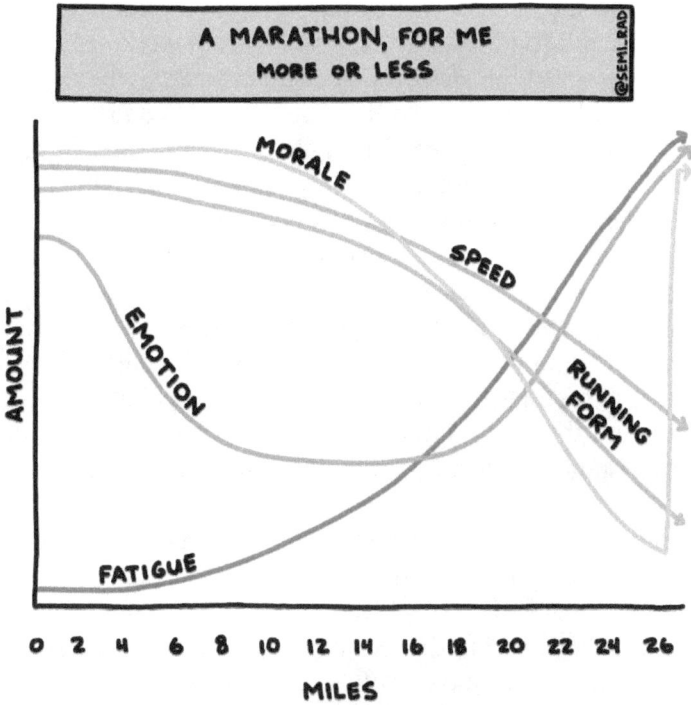

Just after the last turn into Central Park at Columbus Circle, a few people could obviously smell the barn and found an energy reserve, and were able to pick it up for the final one-third mile to the finish line. I was unable to find any such motivation. I felt—and also looked, as the official race photos later confirmed—like someone who had just woken up from a monthlong coma and started wandering around the hospital. If I had looked down and seen that my legs had somehow turned into wood, I would not have been surprised. I jogged across the finish line, stopped my watch, took a quick selfie and texted it to my wife with the words "Hello I am dead" and shuffled along with all the other finishers, through the volunteers handing us bags containing drinks and food. I accepted a post-race poncho from a volunteer, and made my way over to a curb, where I thought I might sit down for a few minutes and chug the Gatorade, recovery drink, and bottle of water in my bag, but when I tried to bend my knees more than 25 degrees in order to sit down, it became clear that I would not be able to get up from that position.

So I kept shuffling, joining the almost-silent procession of blue zombies making our way down the park drive to 72nd Street. Heads were down, no one was talking, because they were either too tired or because they were texting their people about their finish and/or where to meet up to sit on furniture and consume calories immediately upon exiting the park. I checked the app to see where Syd was, and he was only a few minutes behind me. At 72nd and Central Park West, long rows of benches lined both sides of the drive, and I found a spot behind a group of police officers and gingerly lowered myself halfway down, then plopped onto the bench. For a second, I thought I might be able to wrap myself up in the poncho and sleep here for a few hours.

After a few minutes, Syd appeared, walking up the drive, looking no worse for wear than when I'd seen him a few miles ago. He asked how I felt, if I finished in under four hours, and then said, "I popped my hamstring twice in the last quarter mile." I said "Uhhhh what, is it really painful?" He said, still half-smiling, "oh yeah." We stopped in front of the last official race photographer to get our photo together, and then walked out of the park, heading for the medical tent to get some ice. Syd said, "That was the dumbest thing I've ever done, and it was also the most amazing thing I've ever done." And then:

"I think I realized today that I don't need to do any other races—this is the greatest race in the world." I understood what he meant. He just loves the experience—the crowds, the city, the runners, the whole journey. But I simultaneously thought, "That is exactly the kind of attitude that pushes you to the point where you think it's OK to injure yourself in the last 400 meters of your slowest marathon ever, Syd." And honestly, I have a hard time blaming him.

If you enjoyed this book, please consider writing a brief review online, which, if you think about it, is kind of a way of sharing it with people you may never meet, who might also enjoy it.

Brendan Leonard is a columnist at *Outside*, and his writing has appeared in *Runner's World*, *National Geographic Adventure*, *Climbing*, *Alpinist*, and on CNN.com and in dozens of other publications. He directed the 2017 short film How to Run 100 Miles, which screened at film festivals in more than 20 countries and on six continents and was viewed more than 5 million times online. He is the author of *I Hate Running and You Can Too*, *Surviving the Great Outdoors*, and *Sixty Meters to Anywhere*. Find more of his work at Semi-Rad.com.

www.ingramcontent.com/pod-product-compliance
Lightning Source LLC
Chambersburg PA
CBHW022049290426
44109CB00014B/1033